LITERATURE MADE EASY

JOHN STEINBECK'S

OF MICE AND MEN

LITERATURE MADE EASY

JOHN STEINBECK'S

OF MICE AND MEN

Written by RUTH COLEMAN
WITH TONY BUZAN

BARRON'S

First edition for the United States and Canada published by Barron's Educational Series, Inc., 1999.

First published in the United Kingdom by Hodder & Stoughton Ltd. under the title:
A Guide to Of Mice and Men

Cover photograph © The Ronald Grant Archive
Mind Maps: David Orr
Illustrations: Karen Donnelly

Ruth Coleman asserts the moral right to be identified as the author of this work.

American text edited by Benjamin Griffith

All inquiries should be addressed to:
Barron's Educational Series, Inc.
250 Wireless Boulevard
Hauppauge, New York 11788
http://www.barronseduc.com

International Standard Book No. 0-7641-0820-4
Library of Congress Catalog Card No. 98-73078

PRINTED IN THE UNITED STATES OF AMERICA
987654321

CONTENTS

There are five important things you must know about your brain and memory to revolutionize the way you study:

- ◆ how your memory ("recall") works *while* you are learning
- ◆ how your memory works *after* you have finished learning
- ◆ how to use Mind Maps – a special technique for helping you with all aspects of your studies
- ◆ how to prepare for tests and exams.

Recall during learning
– THE NEED FOR BREAKS

When you are studying, your memory can concentrate, understand, and remember well for between 20 and 45 minutes at a time, then it needs a break. If you continue for longer than this without a break, your memory starts to break down. If you study for hours nonstop, you will remember only a small fraction of what you have been trying to learn, and you will have wasted hours of valuable time.

So, ideally, *study for less than an hour*, then take a five- to ten-minute break. During the break listen to music, go for a walk, do some exercise, or just daydream. (Daydreaming is a necessary brain-power booster – geniuses do it regularly.) During the break your brain will be sorting out what it has been learning, and you will go back to your books with the new information safely stored and organized in your memory. We recommend breaks at regular intervals as you work through this book. Make sure you take them!

Recall after learning
— THE WAVES OF YOUR MEMORY

What do you think begins to happen to your
memory right after you have finished learning something?
Does it immediately start forgetting? No! Your brain actually
increases its power and continues remembering. For a short
time after your study session, your brain integrates the
information, making a more complete picture of everything it
has just learned. Only then does the rapid decline in memory
begin, and as much as 80 percent of what you have learned can
be forgotten in a day.

However, if you catch the top of the wave of your memory,
and briefly review (look back over) what you have been
studying at the correct time, the memory is imprinted far more
strongly, and stays at the crest of the wave for a much longer
time. To maximize your brain's power to remember, take a few
minutes at the end of a day and use a Mind Map to review
what you have learned. Then review it at the end of a week,
again at the end of a month, and finally a week before your
test or exam. That way you'll ride your memory
wave all the way there – and beyond!

The Mind Map ®
— A PICTURE OF THE WAY YOU THINK

Do you like taking notes? More important, do you like having to
go back over and learn them before tests or exams? Most
students I know certainly do not! And how do you take your
notes? Most people take notes on lined paper, using blue or
black ink. The result, visually, is boring. And what does *your*
brain do when it is bored? It turns off, tunes out, and goes to
sleep! Add a dash of color, rhythm, imagination, and the whole
note-taking process becomes much more fun, uses more of your
brain's abilities, and improves your recall and understanding.

Generally, your Mind Map is highly personal and need not be
understandable to any other person. It mirrors *your* brain. Its
purpose is to build up your "memory muscle" by creating
images that will help you recall instantly the most important
points about the characters and plot sequences in a work of
fiction you are studying.

HOW TO DRAW A MIND MAP

1 First of all, briefly examine the Mind Maps and Mini Mind Maps used in this book. What are the common characteristics? All of them use small pictures or symbols, with words branching out from the illustration.

2 Decide which idea or character in the book you want to illustrate and draw a picture, starting in the middle of the page so that you have plenty of room to branch out. Remember that no one expects a young Rembrandt or Picasso here; artistic ability is not as important as creating an image you (and you alone) will remember. A round smiling (or sad) face might work as well in your memory as a finished portrait. Use marking pens of different colors to make your Mind Map as vivid and memorable as possible.

3 As your thoughts flow freely, add descriptive words and other ideas on the colored branching lines that connect to the central image. Print clearly, using one word per line if possible.

4 Further refine your thinking by adding smaller branching lines, containing less important facts and ideas, to the main points.

5 Presto! You have a personal outline of your thoughts about the character and plot. It's not a stiff formal outline, but a colorful image that will stick in your mind, it is hoped, throughout classroom discussions and final exams.

HOW TO READ A MIND MAP

1 Begin in the center, the focus of your topic.

2 The words/images attached to the center are like chapter headings; read them next.

3 Always read out from the center, in every direction (even on the left-hand side, where you will have to read from right to left, instead of the usual left to right).

USING MIND MAPS

Mind Maps are a versatile tool; use them for taking notes in class or from books, for solving problems, for brainstorming with friends, and for reviewing and working for tests or exams – their uses are endless! You will find them invaluable for planning essays for coursework and exams. Number your main branches in the order in which you want to use them and off you go – the main headings for your essay are done and all your ideas are logically organized.

Preparing for tests and exams

◆ Review your work systematically. Study hard at the beginning of your course, not the end, and avoid "exam panic."
◆ Use Mind Maps throughout your course, and build a Master Mind Map for each subject – a giant Mind Map that summarizes everything you know about the subject.
◆ Use memory techniques such as mnemonics (verses or systems for remembering such things as dates and events).
◆ Get together with one or two friends to study, compare Mind Maps, and discuss topics.

AND FINALLY...

Have *fun* while you learn – it has been shown that students who make their studies enjoyable understand and remember everything better and get the highest grades. I wish you and your brain every success! (Tony Buzan)

HOW TO USE THIS GUIDE

This guide assumes that you have already read *Of Mice and Men*, although you could read Background and *Of Mice and Men* – the Story before that. It is best to use the guide alongside the text. You could read the Who's Who? and Themes sections without referring to the novel, but you will get more out of these sections if you do refer to it to check the points made, and especially when thinking about the questions designed to test your recall and help you think about the novel.

The different sections

The Commentary section can be used in a number of ways. One way is to read a chapter or part of a chapter in the novel, and then read the commentary for that section. Continue until you come to a test yourself exercise – **then take a break**! Or, read the Commentary for a chapter or part of a chapter, then read that section in the novel, then go back to the Commentary. Find out what works best for you.

Topics for Discussion and Brainstorming lists topics that could well appear on exams or provide the basis for coursework. It would be particularly useful for you to discuss them with friends, or brainstorm them using Mind Map techniques (see p. viii).

How to Get an "A" in English Literature explains what to look for in a text and what skills you need to develop to achieve a lifelong appreciation of literature.

The Exam Essay is a useful night-before reminder of how to tackle exam questions, and the Model Answer and Essay Plan gives an example of an "A"-grade essay and the Mind Map and plan used to write it.

The questions

Whenever you come across a question in the guide with a star ✪ in front of it, think about it for a moment. You could even jot down a few words to focus your mind. There is not usually a "right" answer to these questions; it is important for you to develop your own opinions. The Test Yourself sections are designed to take you about 10–20 minutes each – which will be time well spent. Take a short break after each one.

KEY TO ICONS

Themes

A **theme** is an idea explored by an author. Whenever a theme is dealt with in the guide, the appropriate icon is used. This means you can find where a theme is mentioned just by flicking through the book. Try it now.

Broken dreams   Friendship

Inequality   Loneliness

These themes are interrelated. Characters without friends are lonely. The friendship between George and Lennie is based on their dreams for a better life. Inequality can be perceived differently: the Boss and Curley have power, but are inferior to Slim, whose skill and personal qualities gain respect.

LANGUAGE, STYLE, AND STRUCTURE

This icon is used whenever the guide focuses on the author's choice of words and **imagery** (a kind of word picture used to make an idea come alive) and the overall way in which the novel is organized.

This short novel is tightly structured in six scenes, with the last five containing a significant event, or climax. The novel begins and ends with a scene at the same location, giving the story cyclical form.

Facts about the American Depression

1929 — ST. VALENTINE'S DAY MASSACRE, CHICAGO. BUGSY MORAN'S GANG GUNNED DOWN

1933 — FIRST DRIVE IN MOVIE THEATER OPENS IN NEW JERSEY.

COLLAPSE OF NEW YORK STOCK MARKET 1.5 MILLION UNEMPLOYED

1934 — NYLON INVENTED. STOCKINGS CAME LATER

FIRST LAUNDERETTE OPENS IN TEXAS

DONALD DUCK MAKES FIRST FILM APPEARANCE

1930 — 3 MILLION UNEMPLOYED

1935 — BEER CANS INTRODUCED

ALCOHOLICS ANONYMOUS FOUNDED IN OHIO

SLICED BREAD INTRODUCED

1936 — FLUORESCENT LIGHTING INTRODUCED

FIRST POP MUSIC CHART COMPILED IN NEW YORK

1931 — EMPIRE STATE BUILDING COMPLETED, NEW YORK

2,298 BANKS COLLAPSE

1937 — GOLDEN GATE BRIDGE, SAN FRANCISCO OPENS

1932 — 13 MILLION UNEMPLOYED. RED CROSS GIVES 75 CENTS PER WEEK TO STARVING FAMILIES

BEGUN IN 1936 OF MICE AND MEN IS PUBLISHED

OF MICE AND MEN JOHN STEINBECK

WORKERS MIGRATE

The Depression

Of Mice and Men is a short work of fiction, often referred to as a novella or novelette. Set in California, during the early to mid 1930s, *Of Mice and Men* is John Steinbeck's compassionate story of the harsh realities of life for poor unskilled workers displaced by the Depression – a period of economic decline and high unemployment in (Western industrialized nations). In America, the Depression began abruptly in October 1929 and lasted into the mid 1930s. Briefly a ranch hand himself, most of Steinbeck's early and best work was concerned with social issues of the day. Such works include *Of Mice and Men* and *The Grapes of Wrath*.

Steinbeck's presentation of the poor

People disagree about the literary influences that contributed to Steinbeck's style. He did, however, depart from many of the conventions that had characterized American literature in the 1920s when times were more prosperous. His sympathetic presentation of the poor and disadvantaged made him extremely unpopular with exploitative employers and landowners whom he held responsible for perpetuating the cycle of poverty and deprivation.

How the book evolved

Of Mice and Men went through several stages of development before it reached the form we read today. Completed in 1936, early drafts took long to write because Steinbeck felt that he needed plenty of time to tell the story in a way that would not patronize or exploit the people he was writing about.
A further delay occurred when half the manuscript was destroyed by Steinbeck's dog and had to be rewritten.

In its early form the book was called *Something That Happened* – a matter-of-fact title that reflects its content as a work concerned with presenting people and the events that shape their lives as they are, rather than analyzing why it should be. Steinbeck deliberately intended to write the story in such a way that it could become a play with little adaptation.

Steinbeck did not expect *Of Mice and Men* to be the enormous success it proved to be. He had struggled as a writer with little else published before he wrote it at the age of 34. It proved to be the work that propelled the young Steinbeck to fame, although nearly 30 years were to pass before he was awarded the Nobel Prize for Literature. The final product, *Of Mice and Men*, published in 1937, was named after a poem by Robert Burns called *To a Mouse, on Turning up Her Nest with the Plough*. The relevant lines are:

> *The best-laid schemes o' mice and men*
> *Gang aft a-gley [often go wrong],*
> *And lea'e us nought but grief and pain*
> *For promised joy.*

The title reflects the way in which living things are often powerless to face forces greater than themselves. ✪ Do you think it was a good choice?

Summary

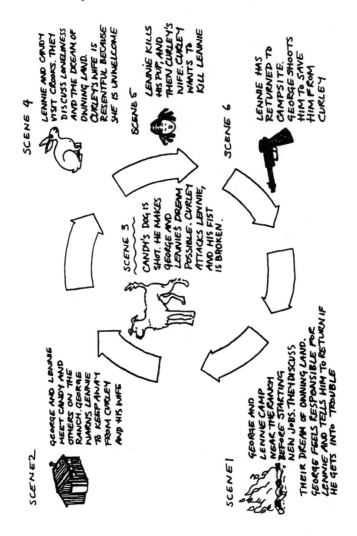

SCENE 4

LENNIE AND CANDY VISIT CROOKS. THEY DISCUSS LONELINESS AND THE DREAM OF OWNING LAND. CURLEY'S WIFE IS RESENTFUL BECAUSE SHE IS UNWELCOME

SCENE 5

LENNIE KILLS HIS PUP, AND THEN CURLEY'S WIFE. CURLEY WANTS TO KILL LENNIE

SCENE 6

LENNIE HAS RETURNED TO CAMPSITE. GEORGE SHOOTS HIM TO SAVE HIM FROM CURLEY

SCENE 3

CANDY'S DOG IS SHOT. HE MAKES GEORGE AND LENNIE'S DREAM POSSIBLE. CURLEY ATTACKS LENNIE, AND HIS FIST IS BROKEN.

SCENE 2

GEORGE AND LENNIE MEET CANDY AND OTHERS ON THE RANCH. GEORGE WARNS LENNIE TO KEEP AWAY FROM CURLEY AND HIS WIFE

SCENE 1

GEORGE AND LENNIE CAMP NEAR THE RANCH BEFORE STARTING NEW JOBS. THEY DISCUSS THEIR DREAM OF OWNING LAND. GEORGE FEELS RESPONSIBLE FOR LENNIE AND TELLS HIM TO RETURN IF HE GETS INTO TROUBLE

3

George and Lennie introduced

The story is set in **California**, during the **Great Depression.** Two **migrant** workers and friends, George **Milton** and Lennie **Small**, sit around a campfire close to the **ranch** where they will start new **jobs** in the morning. They dream of **owning** land. It becomes clear that **George** feels a great burden of responsibility for **Lennie**, who is slow and simple. George tells Lennie to **return** to the campsite and wait for him if he gets into any trouble.

Meeting the other characters

At the ranch the pair meet **Candy,** who cleans the communal dormitory. They are soon introduced to the **boss** and his son, **Curley**, who is **small** and **aggressive**, and takes a dislike to Lennie, who is big. George tells Lennie to keep away from Curley and his pretty new **wife**, who constantly looks for company. Slim, a **supervisor**, has a dog with **puppies** and he gives one to Lennie. George **confides** to Slim that where they last **worked**, Lennie innocently **touched** a girl's **dress** and wouldn't let go. He was **accused** of rape, and so the two friends ran away.

Curley picks a fight

Candy reluctantly allows his **dog** to be **shot** because it is **old** and smelly. The old man **listens** to George and Lennie talking about their dream of owning **land** and says he has **savings** that make the idea possible. They decide to go ahead as a threesome. As Lennie **laughs** with pleasure at the idea, Curley **attacks** him. Lennie **strikes** back only when **George** instructs him to. Again he won't **let** go, and his strength is so **great** that he breaks **Curley's** fist.

Lennie and Candy **visit** Crooks the **black** stablehand and **discuss** their plan with him. Curley's wife also visits Crooks and is **resentful** because she is so unwelcome.

Lennie kills Curley's wife

The next day Lennie is in the **barn** grieving over his **puppy** that he has **accidentally** killed. He is **joined** by Curley's **lonely** wife, who **dreams** of being in the movies. Because Lennie likes to touch **soft** things, she **invites** him to touch her hair. In a **repeat** of the incident with the girl's **dress** and Curley's **fist**, Lennie **panics** and won't let go. Not realizing his own **strength**, Lennie breaks her **neck** and **kills** her. As the **death** is discovered, Lennie **returns** to the campsite. George **steals** a gun, goes to the campsite, and **shoots** Lennie himself to **save** him from the **savage** Curley.

HOW MUCH CAN YOU REMEMBER?

Without looking back, try filling in the missing words or use your own to summarize the story. Then check how you've done.

George and Lennie introduced

The story is set in _____, during the _____ _____. Two _____ workers and friends, George _____ and Lennie _____, sit around a campfire close to the _____ where they will start new _____ in the morning. They dream of _____ land. It becomes clear that _____ feels a great burden of responsibility for _____, who is slow and simple. George tells Lennie to _____ to the campsite and wait for him if he gets into any trouble.

Meeting the other characters

At the ranch the pair meet _____, who cleans the communal dormitory. They are soon introduced to the _____ and his son, _____, who is _____ and _____, and takes a dislike to Lennie, who is big. George tells Lennie to keep away from Curley and his pretty new _____, who constantly looks for company. Slim, a _____, has a dog with _____ and he gives one to Lennie. George _____ to Slim that where they last _____, Lennie innocently _____ a girl's _____ and wouldn't let go. He was _____ of rape, and so the two friends ran away and escaped.

Curley picks a fight

Candy reluctantly allows his _____ to be _____ because it is _____ and smelly. The old man _____ to George and Lennie talking about their dream of owning _____ and says he has _____ that make the idea

5

possible. They decide to go ahead as a threesome. As Lennie _____ with pleasure at the idea, Curley _____ him. Lennie _____ back only when _____ instructs him to. Again he won't _____ go, and his strength is so _____ that he breaks _____ fist.

Lennie and Candy _____ Crooks the _____ stablehand and _____ their plan with him. Curley's wife also visits Crooks and is _____ because she is so unwelcome.

Lennie kills Curley's wife

The next day Lennie is in the _____ grieving over his _____ that he has _____ killed. He is _____ by Curley's _____ wife, who _____ of being in the movies. Because Lennie likes to touch _____ things, she _____ him to touch her hair. In a _____ of the incident with the girl's _____ and Curley's _____, Lennie _____ and won't let go. Not realizing his own _____, Lennie breaks her _____ and _____ her. As the _____ is discovered, Lennie _____ to the campsite. George _____ a gun, goes to the campsite, and _____ Lennie himself to _____ him from the _____ Curley.

Now try to complete this picture with a text summary. (Look back to p. 3 if you need a reminder.)

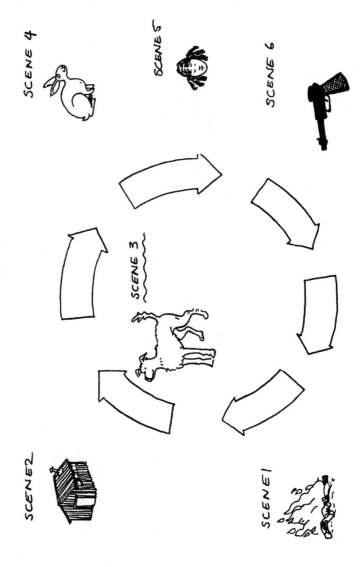

Lennie Small

Lennie the migrant worker is a gentle giant who has a learning
disability. His childlike interest in animals, loyalty to his friend
George, his sweet nature, and the tragedy that befalls him
make him an endearing character for whom most readers feel a
great deal of sympathy. In contrast to Curley, the character who
emerges as his enemy, Lennie has no mean streak in his nature,
although he is very strong. Steinbeck often uses animal imagery
to describe Lennie, and it is **ironic** that his last name is Small
because he is a very big man.

Lennie's relationship with George

That Lennie is a follower rather than a leader is apparent
from the very first mention of him. He trusts George so
completely that he walks along behind him even in open
spaces, and when his companion stops walking, almost bumps
into him. This hints at what is soon revealed – that Lennie
relies on George to show the way in everything. He cannot
think for himself and forgets most things quickly.

Although Lennie is simple and forgetful, he is not emotionally
unaware. He realizes that he is sometimes a burden to George
and would rather go his own way than stay if he is not wanted.

He is quick to pick up on the bad atmosphere at the ranch, and almost senses his own fate when he says: *"I don't like this place, George. This ain't no good place. I wanna get outa here."* ✪ How do you think Lennie would manage on his own?

Although George complains about feeling responsible for Lennie, there is much evidence that he depends on Lennie as much as Lennie depends on him. Look at George's conversations with Slim to see this. George's deep understanding of Lennie and kind tone toward him most of the time is almost fatherly. ✪ Do you think Lennie is childlike? Find an example from the text to support your view.

The rabbits

If there is one thing in life that Lennie cares about other than George, it is rabbits, but apart from the rabbits that *come out of the brush to sit on the sand in the evening* at the start of the story, we never actually come across a real one. They are frequently mentioned by Lennie, however, because for him they are a symbol of a better life. He asks for no more than to be able to feed them alfalfa. Lennie pesters George so often to tell him about the *future rabbits* and how it will be his job to tend them that talk of rabbits is an escape for both of them. George tells it to him like a parent telling a child a fairy tale.

So simple is his understanding of crime and punishment that Lennie's first fear when he does something wrong is that George won't let him tend the rabbits. George uses this fear as a way of controlling and setting limits on Lennie's behavior. It is the most successful threat of all to make Lennie remember things such as not to say a word on arriving at the ranch in case his simplemindedness costs them the much-needed jobs. ✪ What other example can you think of?

When Lennie returns to the same location as the real rabbits at the start of the book, *a gigantic rabbit* appears out of his head. It is a figment of Lennie's imagination, conjured up by his guilt about Curley's wife, and his anticipated rejection by George. It is a sad moment in the book when the rabbit says: *"You ain't fit to lick the boots of no rabbit. You'd forget to feed 'em and let 'em go hungry."* ✪ Do you think Lennie would forget?

Lennie's strength is his downfall

Lennie carries a dead mouse that he has probably accidentally killed while petting it. His love for soft things and tendency to grip too tightly has gotten him into trouble before we join the story. In a town called Weed where they last worked, he innocently touched a girl's dress, held on tightly, and frightened her until she *squawked*. The incident resulted in a false rape charge and a manhunt that forced the two to move on to a new part of California. This is an example of **foreshadowing**. It warns us of what is to come – the sad repetition of the incident with Curley's wife later in the book. We also witness the effect of Lennie's vice-like grip when he damages Curley's hand and when he accidentally kills his puppy.

George Milton

George is described as *small and quick, dark of face, with restless eyes and sharp, strong features,* with *small, strong hands, slender arms, a thin and bony nose.* Notice the repetition of "small" in this description; it contrasts with the largeness of Lennie.

Relationship with Lennie

George's character does not show to its best advantage at first because he is angry with the bus driver who dropped them off in the wrong place and because he is irritated with Lennie. They have been run out of Weed because of Lennie, have been constantly in each other's company, and when he stopped walking, Lennie *nearly ran over* him. ✪ Do you think such a companion would get on your nerves?

In the opening pages Steinbeck makes it clear that George has helped his companion out of many scrapes. He even carries Lennie's work card for him because he cannot be trusted to look after it properly himself. George also thinks about food for both of them.

His friendship with Lennie has not always been as watchful and caring, however. When George confides in Slim, who describes him as *a smart little guy*, we learn that he used to *play jokes* on Lennie, because *he was too dumb to take care of 'imself. But he was fun. Made me seem God damn smart alongside of him.* Lennie almost drowned because George told him to jump in the river, not realizing he couldn't swim. George did not do it again. ✪ What do you think George's admission to Slim says about him?

Although George is irritable with Lennie, he is also quite proud of him. The evidence of this can be found when he first meets Slim and tells him how strong and capable a worker Lennie is, and again when Slim has witnessed Lennie at work and comments that he has *never seen such a strong guy.*

George's relationships with other people

George makes a confidante of Slim and has other people to talk to and relax with. He is readily accepted by everyone on the ranch, and even Curley leaves him alone. Although the dream of owning his own land is shattered by the death of Curley's wife at Lennie's hands, old Candy has enough respect and affection for George to help him by concealing the fact that George already knows she is dead. It is one of few comforts at the end of the book that George has developed a good relationship with Slim – someone to comfort him in his grief at what he feels he has to do to Lennie.

The shared dream

George, like Lennie, is alone in the world. They got *kinda used to each other after a little while,* and as they recite in the opening and closing scene at the campsite, they have each other. This mutual dependency is the basis for the sharing of their dream to live off the *fatta the lan'*.

Whether George likes it or not, their lives are completely bound up together.

George's personal qualities

Despite his annoyance with Lennie, George has many excellent qualities, and grows in stature throughout the story. He begins as a resentful but responsible care-giver for Lennie, and develops into a man who could restrain himself from

spending money idly in the interests of organizing the
smallholding – a task of which he is more than capable. This
shows that he has drive and commitment. He is clean-living
and retains his self-respect despite his migrant lifestyle. He
does not allow Lennie to drink contaminated water at the
beginning of the story and worries about lice at the
bunkhouse.

George thinks ahead, spots potential danger, knows how to
keep out of trouble, and does not seek it. At the end he shows
great generosity and selflessness by taking the only course
possible with Lennie. He cares for him and recognizes that he
has no choice but to shoot Lennie.

What do you think?

?   We are not told in the story, but how old do you think
      George and Lennie are and why?

?   Do you think George is right to shoot Lennie? Make a
      Mini Mind Map of your thoughts on this.

?   How would George's life be affected by Lennie's
      death? Describe George's life as you think it would be
      after Lennie's death.

*now reward yourself with a break before
reading about an old gossip*

Candy

Candy the bunkhouse cleaner, or *swamper* as he is called in the
book, is a good-natured old gossip. He is a source of
information about all the characters on the ranch and knows
what is going on. He is a useful **device** both for this scene-
setting reason and for providing a way to turn the dream into a
realizable goal because he has savings.

Candy demonstrates what happens to lonely men on
ranches as they grow older. That he has had a farm
accident and lost his hand also makes a point about health and

safety standards on ranches during the Depression when workers were cheap and plentiful. Itinerant workers in 1930s America had no job security, social security, or pension plan. Perhaps it was because Steinbeck wanted to treat even ranch owners fairly that conditions on this ranch seem reasonable and that Candy has some compensation for the injury.

As George discovers, dreams such as theirs only really develop when more than one person is involved. George and Lennie's youthfulness and energy are an answer to the problem of old age for Candy who, like most workers, has no family.

Candy serves another useful purpose. He is fond of his dog even though it is old and smelly. He is rushed into allowing Carlson to shoot it and is too upset to do it himself, which he quickly regrets. Candy soon makes a confession that provides a parallel to George's dilemma about shooting Lennie himself or leaving Curley to savage him. ✪ What does Candy say to George that demonstrates his regret?

Curley

Curley, the boss's son, is a vicious bully and a coward. He is described as *a thin young man with a brown face, with brown eyes and a head of tightly curled hair*. Like his father he wears the high-heeled boots that distinguish him from working men. He has enjoyed some success as a boxer.

Liked by no one, not even his wife, Curley is a contrast to the other ranchers, particularly the large Lennie. He is small, aggressive, jealous, mean-spirited and vengeful. He demonstrates that privilege does not necessarily create a kind and generous person. These qualities are more apparent in the lowly ranch hands.

His brutal and unprovoked attack on the gentle Lennie immediately follows the scene in which the sympathetic characters realize they have a chance for a good and independent future. It is a reminder that their dream is fated not to come true. ✪ How is Curley's ultimate power and authority demonstrated at the end of the story?

13

OF MICE AND MEN

Curley's wife

Before we meet Curley's wife, Candy criticizes her for giving men other than her husband *the eye*. He also accuses her of being *a tart* and his comments make us start out with a bad impression of her. Steinbeck reinforces this image when he describes her. She has *full, rouged lips and wide-spaced eyes, heavily made up. Her finger-nails were red. Her hair hung in little rolled clusters, like sausages.*

The way she uses her body, and her persistent attempts to look for company by using flimsy excuses for visiting the men's quarters contribute to George's view of her as *a tramp* and *jail bait*, a forbidden temptation that leads to jail. George says such a ranch *ain't no place for a girl, specially like her.* ❸ Do you agree?

Although she is the main reason for the tragedy that befalls Lennie, she is not entirely an unsympathetic character. She makes a poor choice of husband to spite her mother and is left feeling lonely. With no real companionship on the ranch, it is not altogether surprising that she looks for company. Despite her obvious sexual charms, the only weapon she has, the men shun her; their jobs and physical well-being depend on not upsetting the mean and jealous Curley. In this situation her attractiveness is of no use to her whatsoever. It is pathetic that her powerlessness is so great that she wields what little she has in threats to Crooks and Candy. She is in a no-win situation. By definition, as Curley's wife, she is unable to make friends on the ranch.

Steinbeck never names Curley's wife. She is defined by her relationship to Curley, not as an individual. Namelessness also has the effect of reinforcing how insignificant she is in the life of the ranch, how dependent she is on Curley, and how little she is respected by all.

Curley's wife also has dreams that do not come true. She is perhaps pretty enough to be in the movies, a dream shared by countless other young women in the 1930s. She believes that if only she had received a letter from a man who made her promises, her dream would have come true, and she would not have made the mistake of marrying Curley. The tragedy that cuts short her miserable life is a release.

Now try this

? How does Candy hope to help out on the small piece of land he provides the deposit for?

? What do you think of Curley and the way he treats his wife?

? There is evidence in the text to suggest that Curley's wife will be happier in death than she has been in life. Where in the text is this suggested?

Slim

Slim, the jerkline skinner, or supervisor in charge of steering horse- or mule-drawn carts, is universally respected. Steinbeck's description of his skill and personal qualities is more full of praise than it is for any other character. ❍ Jot down some of the other statements Steinbeck uses to praise him.

Slim's main purpose in the story is to set the moral tone of the bunkhouse and to demonstrate that self-respect and noble qualities can be found in the lowly. He is an ally to the downtrodden ranch hands and ensures that justice is done. ❍ How does this show in the deal he strikes up with Curley after Lennie has crushed his fist?

Slim is kind enough to give Lennie a puppy; he recognizes Lennie's true nature and supports George in his difficulties with his friend. He treats George with a respect that draws confidences from him. Candy accepts the death of his dog because Slim agrees the time has come, and even Curley apologizes for suspecting he is having an affair with his wife. Slim is the one who reminds Carlson to bury the dog and makes the arrangements to send Curley to the doctor. All the other characters look up to him: *His authority was so great that his word was taken on any subject, be it politics or love.* Even so, his authority is not great enough to be able to restrain the powerful Curley from seeking out Lennie at the end. Slim also thinks that it would be kinder to shoot Lennie than to lock him up in jail. ✪ What are your views on this?

When Slim first appears in the story we are relieved that someone is on George and Lennie's side against the powerful ranch-owning family we have just met. By the end of the story, we respect Slim as much as the other characters do. His comment in support of George's action in shooting Lennie: "*You hadda, George. I swear you hadda*," has the effect of defending the action to the reader as well as to George.

Crooks

With a nickname derived from the crooked back he has suffered since a horse kicked him, Crooks the stablehand is the only African-American person in the book. Described by Candy as *a nice fella*, he is the victim of racial prejudice and the main recipient of unequal treatment. The first we hear of him is that when the boss is angry he takes it out on Crooks simply because of his race. He is not allowed in the bunkhouse, but is tolerated when playing games outside. Even when he is allowed into the bunkhouse out of Christmas cheer, Crooks ends up the victim of a fight.

Steinbeck makes us aware of Crooks' inner feelings to demonstrate the unfairness with which he is treated, and to make us understand and sympathize with his isolation. He has managed to carve out some kind of life for himself, however, despite his disadvantage. He has more possessions than the others have because a stablehand's job is more permanent, he is good at his job, and wins at horseshoes, a game that involves throwing horseshoes over a stake in the ground.

Like so many other characters in the story, Crooks is desperately lonely. We learn this when first Lennie, and then Candy join him. He displays a dignified reluctance to allow other people into his room since he is not invited into theirs, but is secretly delighted to play host to Lennie and Candy.

In his jealousy of their close friendship, Crooks rather spitefully teases Lennie that George may not return from the Saturday night partying that all the other workers are indulging in. He soon warms to the frightened Lennie, however, and although he is a cynic who does not believe in happy endings, even he, for a moment, is caught up in the dream of owning land.

When Curley's wife enters his room, the four most powerless characters in the novel are all together. Although they have much in common, they do not find solace in each other's company. Instead, the presence of Curley's wife causes anger and tension. Crooks is powerless because of his race, Lennie because of his learning disabilities, Candy because of his old age, and Curley's wife because she is a woman, married to a man with ultimate power over them all. As she complains to them of her loneliness, Steinbeck describes Crooks as retiring *into the terrible protective dignity of the negro.* ❂ What do you think Steinbeck means by this?

The boss

Another character who is never given a name, his main function seems to be to set the hard, no-nonsense tone of the ranch and to demonstrate to George, Lennie, and the reader the meanness that can be expected there. His suspicion that George is exploiting Lennie paves the way for Curley's behavior.

Carlson

Carlson's main involvement in the story is to bully Candy into parting with his old dog and to back Curley in his hunt for Lennie. He does not display the vicious streak that Curley has, but is the kind of character that, like Whit, can be relied upon to join in any action when it occurs. He is so insensitive and his understanding of human nature so limited that when George and Slim leave the site of Lennie's death, he says: *"Now what the hell ya suppose is eatin' them two guys?"* Like Whit, Carlson typifies a certain type of ranch hand – tough, bullish, unsentimental, and better suited to ranch life because of it.

A NOTE ON NAMES

So called "nicknames" are well used in the book. It is a feature of nicknames that they often pick out and emphasize something about a person. This may be a habit, some aspect of their appearance or manner, or it may be connected to an interest they have or a job they do.

❂ Which characters in the story have nicknames, and how have these names come about? Perhaps you could draw up a Mind Map to help you.

Of all the characters we meet, only George and Lennie are given both a first name and a last name. Some of the characters have no name at all. Curley's wife is deprived of an individual identity by not being named. She is defined solely by her relationship to Curley. The boss does not really need a name. He appears only briefly to set the tone of the ranch, and no one is in any doubt about who he is and what he does.

Over to you

?   Pick out some examples of the characters' actions and words that demonstrate how much respect they have for Slim.

?   How fair is the fight between Crooks and Smitty that Candy describes?

?   What characteristics does Curley share with his father?

?   Which character do you like most? Why?

?   Which character do you like least? Why?

study the Mind Map opposite for a picture summary of who's who... then take a break.

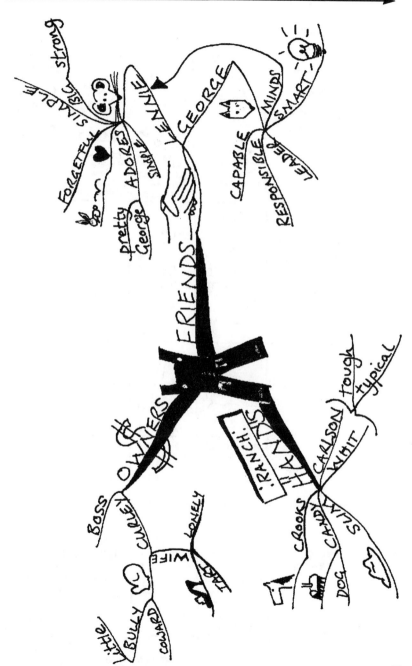

THEME	CHARACTERS INVOLVED IN DEVELOPING THEMES			
 BROKEN DREAMS	 <u>GEORGE</u> WANTS OWN LAND. DREAM DIES WITH LENNIE	 <u>LENNIE</u> WANTS RABBITS ON OWN LAND WITH GEORGE. KILLS AND IS KILLED	 <u>CANDY</u> WANTS LAND WITH GEORGE AND LENNIE. DREAM DIES WITH LENNIE	 CURLEY'S WIFE DREAMS OF BEING IN MOVIES BUT LENNIE KILLS HER
 FRIENDSHIP	 <u>GEORGE</u> LOOKS AFTER BUT ALSO DEPENDS ON LENNIE	 <u>LENNIE</u> DEPENDS ON GEORGE FOR EVERYTHING		
 LONELINESS	 <u>CROOKS</u> AFRICAN-AMERICAN VICTIM OF RACIAL DISCRIMINATION	 <u>CANDY</u> NO FAMILY, GETTING OLD. DOG KILLED	 CURLEY'S WIFE BAD HUSBAND, NO COMPANY	
 INEQUALITY	 <u>CANDY</u> OLD AND DISABLED	 <u>CROOKS</u> AFRICAN-AMERICAN AND DISABLED SUFFERS DISCRIMINATION	 CURLEY'S WIFE FEMALE, VICTIM OF SEXISM	 <u>LENNIE</u> HAS LEARNING DISABILITIES

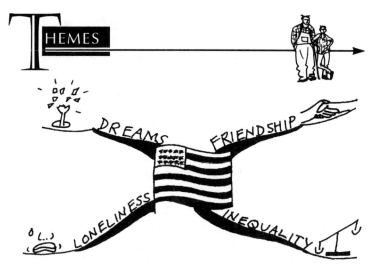

THEMES

A **theme** is an idea developed or explored throughout a work (for example, a play, book, or poem). The main themes in *Of Mice and Men* are shown in the Mini Mind Map above, and can be identified as follows:

- broken dreams
- friendship
- loneliness
- inequality.

Broken dreams

Everyone has dreams, hopes, and ambitions. The characters in *Of Mice and Men* are no different. Rather, because their lives are hard, insecure, and unrewarding, they desperately need dreams to make life worth living. The vivid intensity of their fantasies offsets the misery of real life.

GEORGE AND LENNIE

Nowhere is this truth about human need more pronounced than in George and Lennie's dream of living off the *fatta the lan'*. First introduced when the two are at the campsite the day before taking up new jobs, the idea soothes and comforts Lennie just as a bedtime story comforts a child. He has heard George tell the story of their dream many times and knows it by heart. It is kept alive by being told regularly, and it gives them something to look forward to and to strive for. All Lennie asks for in life is to have warm company and to tend the rabbits.

George is more realistic about life, because he is *a smart little guy.* He understands the harsh realities of his and Lennie's life, and the practical difficulties in the way of achieving their ambition. He is often reluctant to tell Lennie the story of their hoped-for future for these reasons, but enjoys telling it once he starts. As George says to Candy when the dream is over: *"I think I knowed we'd never do her. He usta like to hear about it so much I got to thinking maybe we would."*

Although George is capable of organizing a smallholding and could go ahead without Lennie, he gives up the dream very easily after the death of Curley's wife. Without Lennie to drive him on, George is likely to spend his *stake* on gambling in poolrooms and chasing women as an antidote to hard work – exactly what he says he wishes for when he is frustrated with Lennie.

AND CANDY MAKES THREE

Candy's *greatest fear* is that the dream will evaporate. For him it is the happy answer to having no family, being disabled, and growing old. His savings and willingness to help out briefly put the dream within their grasp. As the three of them discuss it, the dream is embellished with more detail than ever before, and in his delight, Candy spends his time *figurin' about them rabbits* until his simple dream is shattered.

George, Lennie, and Candy dream of having power over their lives, being able to turn away unwelcome visitors, and to warmly greet welcome ones, and to reap what they sow – matters over which they have no control on the ranch. Even Crooks, who has to cope with the added disadvantage of being black in a racially prejudiced community, and who does not dare to have dreams, becomes mesmerized when Lennie and Candy talk about the smallholding. For one brief minute it is his dream too.

It is Crooks who puts George and Lennie's dream in the context of all migrant workers who, as part of a generation who experienced mass unemployment and social upheaval, shared visions of a better future in what became known as the American Dream: *"I see hundreds of men come by on the road an' on the ranches with bindles on their back an' that same damn thing in their heads. Hundreds of them ... nobody never gets no land. It's just in their head."* As Crooks predicts, when Lennie dies, he takes the dream with him.

The other migrant workers also hope for better times. They dream of being the heroes they read about in *those Western magazines ranch-men love to read and scoff at and secretly believe.*

CURLEY'S WIFE

Curley's wife longs for a glamorous life in Hollywood where, at the time the book was written, the film industry was growing and a handful of pretty women went from rags to riches to become movie stars. The naïveté with which she explains away the letter she was promised by a flirtatious man offering her parts in the movies is partly a reluctance to admit the truth to herself. She has to keep the dream alive to have something to live for. With a bad marriage and no company, she is, like Lennie, another tragic character for whom dreams do not come true.

Friendship

For migrant workers, displaced from families broken up by the need to travel for work, and with little hope of settling down to establish their own families on their own land, true and lasting friendships were not common. Against this background, the friendship between George and Lennie is all the more special because it is so rare.

Steinbeck often draws attention to how unusual their friendship is, mainly by making the other characters comment on it. The boss is very suspicious, because he has not seen *one guy take so much trouble for another guy*. He thinks George must be exploiting Lennie by taking away his pay. Curley soon echoes the boss's interest in establishing the nature of the relationship and Crooks is so envious of the friendship that out of spite he upsets Lennie with tales of George deserting him.

Apart from the good-natured Candy, Slim is the only character to understand and support the friendship. At their first meeting he asks if they *travel around together*, and George replies: "*We kinda look after each other.*" As George confides in Slim, he reveals a great deal about the relationship. It is big of George to tell Slim about the incident in which Lennie nearly drowned, because it does not reflect well on him. It does demonstrate Lennie's unflinching loyalty to George, however.

George is frustrated by his friendship with Lennie because he has to think and act for both of them, particularly when Lennie innocently gets into trouble. It annoys George that Lennie forgets most things he has said, except the rabbits. The responsibility of always watching out for Lennie is reduced by having other company on the ranch.

MUTUAL DEPENDENCY

But the two are almost inseparable. George needs Lennie almost as much as Lennie needs George. Like an oath in the form of a chant, they remind themselves at the beginning and the end that "*I got you an' "* ... "*An' I got you.*"

Lennie provides the real driving force behind the dream, and being his keeper gives George the role and direction in life that keeps him from wasting money on transient good times. George also gains confidence in himself by his association with Lennie. He admits to Slim that it makes him look and feel *God damn smart*.

The final demonstration of the noble and loyal qualities brought out of a person by true friendship is that George shoots Lennie to spare him more suffering. It is a repeat of the way in which Candy's old dog is shot in the back of the head by the same gun. The suggestion is that Lennie is like a faithful and loyal dog belonging to George. Unlike Candy, who does not have the courage to kill his dog himself, George ensures that Lennie meets his end painlessly and with dignity by shooting him himself. They go back to where they started at the beginning of the story, having gotten nowhere in between. The problems within their relationship are finally, if sadly, resolved.

Dream on...

?   What does Candy say that expresses his dashed hopes when he looks at Curley's wife's dead body?

?   Do you have a dream? What could stop your dream from being realized? What do your dream and the possible obstacles in the way of it have in common with the dream cherished by George and Lennie?

?   Have you ever had a friend with some of the qualities Steinbeck gives to George or Lennie?

think about it while you take a break

Loneliness

Loneliness runs alongside friendship as a major theme in *Of Mice and Men*. Although ranch life in 1930s America was lonely for migrant workers and many other people, George and Lennie, two of *the loneliest guys in the world*, at least have each other. For African-Americans like Crooks, women like Curley's wife, or the old like Candy, life was far more lonely.

The person who expresses his loneliness most openly and acutely is Crooks the African-American stablehand, a victim of racial prejudice. When Lennie enters his room uninvited, Crooks, out of bitter pride, exercises his only right, that of privacy in his own room. He is so desperately lonely that he cruelly tries to hurt Lennie with tales of George deserting him to try to make him understand what it feels like to be so alone. His envy of their friendship shows when he says: "*George can tell you screwy things, and it don't matter. It's just the talking. It's just bein' with another guy.*"

Glad to have someone to talk to, he warns of the dangers of too much loneliness and continues with: "*A guy needs somebody – to be near him ... A guy goes nuts if he ain't got nobody.*" It is interesting that Steinbeck makes Crooks say the last part of this statement in a whine. It is as if he is a dog pining in its loneliness for the company of its owner. The reason Lennie goes to see Crooks, of course, is

25

that George is out on the town with the other ranch hands and he wants some company. When Candy joins them too, Crooks can hardly *conceal his pleasure with anger.*

Candy the cleaner seems to deal with his loneliness by gossiping and listening for what's going on. He also worries about his future when he is too old to work and explains his reasons for wanting to be part of the plan to buy a smallholding: *"When they can [sack] me here I wisht somebody'd shoot me ... I won't have no place to go, an' I can't get no more jobs."* This is a chilling reminder of the migrant worker's fate in old age.

Curley's wife would have been doomed to an equally lonely old age. In a rash moment brought on by her disappointment at not being in the movies, she marries Curley and soon regrets it. She appears at the door of the bunkhouse and later Crooks's room pretending to be looking for him when she is actually looking for company. As if they can afford to care when their jobs and physical well-being are at stake, she says: *"Think I don't like to talk to somebody ever' once in a while? Think I like to stick in that house alla time?"*

Although Curley's wife likes to flirt, her isolation is genuine: *Sat'iday night. Ever'body out doin' som'pin. Ever'body! An' what am I doin'? Standin' here talking to a bunch of bindle stiffs [tramps with bundles] – an' likin' it because they ain't nobody else.* There is no way out of her alienation from the other characters on the ranch, who are all men. When she develops her ill-fated friendship with Lennie, she tells him she gets *awful lonely,* and, like Crooks, appeals to him to understand how she feels. The way Steinbeck uses **imagery** (word pictures) of sunlight and describes Curley's wife in death illustrates how much better off she is dead than alive.

Steinbeck also finds other ways to develop the theme of loneliness. Soledad, the name of the nearby town, and Crooks's birthplace, means "lonely" in Spanish. The way that George can so often be found playing solitaire, a card game for one player, is a reminder that, as George will soon discover, we are all alone in the end, despite our friendships.

Inequality

Of Mice and Men is sometimes called a "social conscience" novel. It reflects Steinbeck's own early experience of ranch life and chronicles a time of social disintegration and mass unemployment. Employers routinely rewarded the traveling workers with bad pay, insecure work, and hazardous conditions. Much disturbed by this, Steinbeck sought to present the truth about these people's lives in his fiction.

The power of employers and their family members – represented by the boss and Curley in the novel – is never far away. The boss makes his position very clear toward the white workers when he is confrontational with George at the interview during his only appearance in the novel. George, Lennie, and Candy all worry about getting the sack. Even the widely respected Slim has no power to influence the vicious and vindictive Curley when he sets out to kill Lennie.

Candy demonstrates the plight of farm workers with disabling injuries who have no family or place to go. He has some financial compensation, but this is useful only if he has someone to care for him. In the 1930s, state-provided social services and homes for older people were virtually nonexistent.

RACIAL PREJUDICE

To be African-American and poor in 1930s America was far worse, however. Racial prejudice from white people toward African-Americans was usual. African-Americans were routinely discriminated against in all areas of life, and they were frequently the victims of violence. Crooks demonstrates this in *Of Mice and Men*. He is ostracized from the bunkhouse, he is abused by the boss regardless of whether he is at fault, and he shares his living quarters with no one. His only consolations are books, an ability to win horseshoe games and handle horses, and a more permanent job than most of the other workers.

We have no doubt that Crooks would be lynched if Curley's wife chose to pick on him. Even at Christmas when Crooks is invited into the bunkhouse, he is picked on for a fight. In a distorted sense of fairness the others see no reason why Crooks should not be their victim just because he is African-American, but ironically, they make allowances for his back injury.

27

SEXUAL DISCRIMINATION

Curley's wife is discriminated against because she is a woman. Few women in the 1930s were able to be economically independent of men, and marriage was really their only option. The nameless woman marries a small-minded man who has no hesitation about leaving her at home on a Saturday night while he probably visits a brothel. He suspects her of being unfaithful and frowns on her attempts to fulfill the basic human need for company. To the workers she is *jail bait*. It is not worth their jobs to talk to her. The bunkhouse is the domain of men only, and there is no female company on the ranch.

Lennie, the *dum-dum* as Curley's wife puts it, lacks the mental ability to exercise control over his massive strength; nor can he act appropriately when he becomes scared or is simply showing playful affection for an animal. He needs George to look after him. He cannot be trusted with his own work card, and he forgets most things quickly. Even in the final scene, when he begins to hallucinate, he still does not fully understand the implications of what he has done. Without George, Lennie's options would simply be jail or a mental institution, referred to by Crooks in colloquial language as a *booby-hatch*. He joins the others in being a character whose futile efforts to create a better life are thwarted by widespread social injustice in 1930s America.

Think about

? What devices does Steinbeck use to reinforce what the characters themselves say about loneliness?

? What would have to be done on the ranch to make life more rewarding for Curley's wife? Make a Mini Mind Map to illustrate your answer.

? What do you think of ranch life in 1930s America? How do you think it might have changed in the decades since the book was written?

? Look at the skeleton picture representing themes and the characters who develop them (on page 29). Can you fill it in without looking back to the completed one on p. 20?

take a break before some style and structure

THEME	CHARACTERS INVOLVED IN DEVELOPING THEMES			
 BROKEN DREAMS	 GEORGE	 LENNIE	 CANDY	 CURLEY'S WIFE
 FRIENDSHIP	 GEORGE	 LENNIE		
 LONELINESS	 CROOKS	 CANDY	 CURLEY'S WIFE	
 **INEQUALITY**	 CANDY	 CROOKS	 CURLEY'S WIFE	 LENNIE

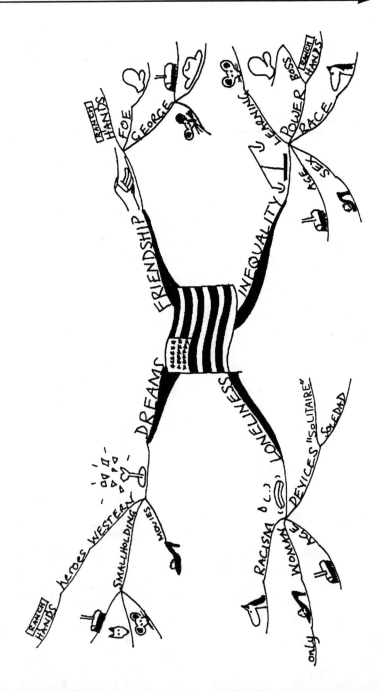

LANGUAGE, STYLE, AND STRUCTURE

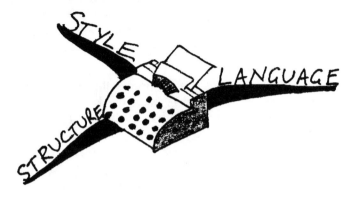

STYLE

LANGUAGE

STRUCTURE

The social and economic reality created by the Great Depression greatly influenced writers such as Steinbeck who were concerned with presenting a true picture of topical issues of the day. By the 1930s, European political demands for social justice and equality for the working classes also began to make themselves felt in America. Before this time, literature had usually reflected the lives of genteel people. Now there emerged a new **realism** and an interest in the lives of the poor. (Realism, in literature, is when an author shows ordinary, everyday details, and makes characters speak and behave as they might in real life.)

This type of realism embodies a sense of fate that determines what happens regardless of anyone's best efforts. Whatever the characters do, they do not have free will, so attempts to improve their lives will prove futile.

Of Mice and Men is written in the **third person**, as if the writer is a fly on the wall; this makes the writer "invisible." The characters are usually only briefly described physically, and demonstrate their inner thoughts by their speech and actions. We are given a private peek into someone's thoughts only once. This is when Lennie hallucinates at the end. ✪ Which technique most accurately reflects real life?

Language

Steinbeck uses simple language to tell a tale of the trials of life for people displaced by the Depression. The dialogue is written in the way it would have been spoken. Lennie speaks in short, simply constructed sentences unless he is copying George's more complex speech. Lennie's sentences are childlike, particularly when he repetitively urges George to tell him the dream story.

Such direct language is characteristic of the uneducated who omit or simplify words and generally break the rules of grammar. To use **double negatives**, such as "*I ain't got no people*" is considered poor use of English.

That these people have a limited vocabulary is clear, but as the boss says, a person doesn't need *any brains to buck barley bags*. ✪ Do you think the use of such language makes the characters more convincing than they otherwise might be?

Most people use some **slang** in their everyday speech; the characters in *Of Mice and Men* are no exception. It is a part of **colloquial language** (ordinary or familiar, rather than formal or literary language). Many slang words are substitutions for other words. In the story these include *jack* for savings, *booby-hatch* for a mental hospital, *canned* for getting the sack, and *bums* or *stiffs* for tramps and hoboes. ✪ What slang words, if any, would you use for these things?

Style

In *Of Mice and Men*, Steinbeck blends a **descriptive style** with a **dramatic style** that is more often found in plays than novels. His use of description shows most clearly in the first and last scenes when he talks of nature and the natural landscape. These descriptions are not essential to the development of the story, whereas all events at the ranch are written economically and with little description. Everything mentioned there has a purpose in developing or echoing a theme or character trait that warns of doom.

The dramatic style that Steinbeck intended from the outset, consists of dialogue that is mainly short exchanges, and it is usually the conversations that develop the story. There are only two main locations, little need for props, only a handful of characters, and plenty of suggestions about how to use light to create symbolic effect – all factors that lend themselves to theater production.

Now try this

?   Flick through the text, and find three examples of double negatives.

?   If you were adapting the novel for the stage, where would you put the intermission and why?

?   With a friend, read aloud some of the dialogue between Crooks and Lennie that begins *Crooks said sharply* ... What do you notice about it?

Imagery

Imagery is the use of words to create pictures, or images, in the reader's mind. Imagery makes what is being said more effective, can make an idea more powerful, or help create a mood. Although *Of Mice and Men* is written in simple language with an economy of style, Steinbeck uses images as **symbols** of things in life. (A symbol is an object used to represent something abstract.) He begins with the winding Salinas River and describes the well-beaten path to the campsite, perhaps in an echo of the journey of life.

Wildlife is referred to only in the opening and closing scenes set by the river. Steinbeck seems to be mentioning them to draw a contrast between the perpetual cycle of nature and a human being's temporary appearance in the scene of life typified by life on the ranch.

Although animals feature prominently in the plot, they are mainly there to draw out the softer, kinder qualities of the tough and downtrodden workers. They also feature in descriptions of people, particularly Lennie. He is compared to a bear and a horse. A little later in the same first scene, Steinbeck compares him to a terrier when he shows extreme reluctance to give up the pet mouse to George. Slim describes Lennie as *a cuckoo*, which implies craziness. Imagery of hands is also well used in this novel. Lennie's are referred to several times as paws, and Curley's gloved fist is significant to the development of the story. ✪ What animal does even Lennie compare himself to at the interview with the boss?

STEINBECK'S USE OF LIGHT

It is significant that Steinbeck often refers to light and dark, or sunshine and shadow as symbols and to create atmosphere. The poor light inside the bunkhouse and Crooks' room reflect the miserable, drab lives of the ranch hands. On the first appearance of Curley's wife in the story, both George and Lennie look up to see that *the rectangle of sunshine in the doorway was cut off*. This chillingly foreshadows (warns us of) the way in which Curley's wife is the eventual cause of Lennie's death and the end of the itinerant duo's dream. ✪ Can you find other examples of the way Steinbeck uses the light and dark inside and outside the bunkhouse to warn the reader of the possibility of better times or of doom?

Such imagery is also used toward the end of the book when Curley's wife and Lennie meet their violent ends. Just before Curley's wife dies, *the light was lifting as the sun went down, and the sun-streaks climbed up the wall* .... After she dies *the sun-streaks* are *high on the wall.* As Lennie's captors advance on him and his fate is sealed: *Already the sun had left the valley to go climbing up the slopes of the Gablilan mountains, and the hill-tops were rosy in the sun.*

As the story moves to its tragic conclusion, ... *the light climbed on out of the valley.* Soon, only *the topmost ridges were in the sun.* Both Lennie and Curley's wife may be happier in death than in life, and this is symbolic of their souls escaping to a better life than they have known on earth. ✪ What judgments might Steinbeck be making about the quality of these two characters by using light against walls for Curley's wife, and mountains for Lennie?

The way in which Steinbeck uses light, and drops clues – for example about Lennie's strength – to hint at what will happen, is sometimes criticized. It is thought that this is making things too obvious for the reader and building up too much sentimentality. ✪ What do you think?

Irony

Irony is is used as a device in language when the opposite of what is really meant is said, or when something turns out in the opposite way to what is intended. An example of irony is when Curley's wife says of her husband, *"Swell guy, ain't he?"* What she actually means is that he is not a swell guy at all, although she appears to suggest that he is. ❂ Can you find a similar example of irony in what Crooks says about his room?

There are several examples of irony when what actually happens, rather than what is said, is opposite to what is intended. Think of the time when Curley's wife and Lennie discuss their dreams in the barn, shortly before they both die. ❂ Where is the irony in George, Lennie, and Candy's dream of *livin' off the fatta the lan'*?

Humor

Of Mice and Men tackles serious themes and issues, but it is not without some humor, such as you might expect from characters who need to relieve the dull monotony of their lives.

Notice the interchange between George and Lennie about colored rabbits near the beginning of the story. ❂ Do you find it amusing? What effect does it have as the closing exchange of the scene?

Now look a little further, when George says *"I ain't mad at you,"* and then instructs Lennie to let Curley *"have it,"* if necessary. ❂ Why is Lennie's reply funny, and what effect does the comment have, coming as it does, between the first meeting with Curley and afterward, with Curley's wife?

Structure

In literature, **structure** refers to the framework for piecing the parts of the work together. This short book has a very tight and defined structure in a cyclical form. The action begins and ends at the same place where the issues raised within the friendship between George and Lennie are introduced and later reach a conclusion. How they arrive at this conclusion is explained in the four scenes that form the four central elements of the story.

The first scene sets the tone, introduces the themes, and gives us an opportunity to get to know and care about the main characters, George and Lennie. Each of the five scenes following contain a climax or significant event. There is the reappearance of Curley at the end of the second part, the shooting of Candy's dog, and the damage to Curley's hand in the third, the confrontation with Curley's wife in the fourth, and her death in the fifth.

The pace of the story is quickened in several ways. The economy of the language and lack of formal chapter breaks increases the sense of immediacy with which all events take place. Nor is any time wasted in shooting either Candy's dog or Lennie.

Ask yourself

? How is imagery of hands used in the final scene?

? When George, Lennie, and Candy embroider the dream of owning land, there is a sense of it becoming real. How does Steinbeck achieve this?

? Do you think the simplicity of Steinbeck's style in this novel attracts or detracts from its seriousness?

? Look at the structural survey opposite. Fill in the boxes when you know the story well enough. Some have already been filled in to help you.

now you've got some style — take a break

Scene 1

Lennie and George introduced.
They are on their way to new jobs.
Lennie gives up dead pet mouse.
George instructs Lennie to keep silent when spoken to at new ranch.
Tensions in the relationship revealed. Some past events mention
Lennie persuades George to tell him about their dream for the future.
George tells Lennie to return and wait if he gets into troub

The story opens with a description of the countryside close to the Salinas River near Soledad in California. All vents take place at or near this place. Steinbeck creates a ense of freshness and hope by setting the story in the spring hen the trees bear new leaves and the wildlife becomes ctive. The animals to be found there become larger, from a zard to deer. There is a sense of the harmony of nature nspoiled by human interference until the dogs belonging to earby ranchers are mentioned.

hat humans inhabit the area is quickly revealed. In an echo o he river mentioned in the first sentence, a path has been eaten nearby. It is perhaps a **metaphor** (see page 76) for comparing life to a river flowing or a road to be traveled.

Those who have beaten the well-used path are clearly at the lower end of the social scale. They are ranch workers and tramps. ✪ How does Steinbeck make sure we know that many such people visit the deep pool under the sycamore tree?

George and Lennie introduced

Evening is falling as the men walk along the path and into the story dressed in denim, the customary clothing of ranch hands. That they carry sleeping blankets tells us that they are next in a long line of transient workers or passersby. The similarity between them ends with their clothes and bedding, and a description of each follows in which the contrast in size, appearance, and manner between Lennie and George is sharply drawn.

We are given our first clue about the nature of the relationship between these two as they are being

---

Structural survey – fill in the boxes with the missing information

Scene	When?	Where?	Who?	What?	Length of scene?
1			George and Lennie		
2	Saturday morning				
3					
4					1–2 hours
5		The bunkhouse			
6				George shoots Lennie	

A Mind Map to summarize Steinbeck's style in *Of Mice and Men*

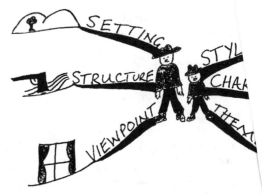

To make reviewing easier, the Commentary d
into scenes, and these scenes into short sectio
with a brief preview that will prepare you for
help with last-minute review. The Commentar
whatever is important in the section, focusing
shown in the Mini Mind Map above.

ICONS

Wherever there is a focus on a particular theme
that theme appears in the margin (see p. xiii for
for the Style and Language sections. Being able
style and language will help you to get an "A" o

You will learn more from the Commentary if you u
the novel itself. Read a section from the novel, th
corresponding Commentary section – or the other

STARRED QUESTIONS

Remember that when a question appears in the Co
with a star ✪ in front of it, you should stop and thin
for a moment. And remember to take a break after
each exercise!

described: *They had walked in single file down the path, and even in the open one stayed behind the other.* Soon after we read that Lennie is so happy to be led without thinking for himself that he nearly bowls George, the *first man* over when he stops walking.

The first words spoken are a warning from George. ✪ Can you find them? The impatient advice he gives to Lennie about unsafe drinking water further emphasizes George's role as his protector. ✪ What else takes place between them to demonstrate that Lennie is dependent on George and that he trusts and admires him?

George and Lennie go to new jobs

George is irritable as he complains that the bus driver was too lazy to take them all the way to the ranch they are heading for. His irritation increases with the revelation that Lennie has forgotten where they are going. The rabbits, the only things that Lennie does seem able to remember, are mentioned for the first time, although no further information about them is given. That George understands the limits of Lennie's capability shows when he reassures Lennie that he has taken responsibility for the work card Lennie thinks he has lost.

Lennie gives up dead mouse

George is quick to notice that Lennie is concealing something when he looks in his pocket for no apparent reason. George takes the dead mouse away from the reluctant Lennie. In a display of childlike innocence, Lennie appeals to George to let him keep it, saying: *"I could pet it with my thumb while we walked along."*

Over to you

? What animals other than the lizard, deer, and ranchers' dogs are mentioned in the opening paragraph? What evidence do they leave to reveal they have been there?

> **?** Describe George and Lennie so far as you know them at this point in the story.

> **?** To which animals is Lennie compared in the opening pages?

take a break before finding out how Lennie likes his beans

George instructs Lennie to keep silent

Lennie further tries George's patience by again forgetting where they are going, but George takes time to be gentle with Lennie to make sure he understands that he must say nothing to his new employer. ✪ Why does George think this is important?

The way in which George briefs Lennie makes us think that it is too much to hope for that Lennie will understand that he must *do no bad things* in the future as he has done in the past at a ranch in a place called Weed. We are not told at this stage what these bad things might be.

Tensions in the relationship revealed

As George settles back to relax, and Lennie gets on his nerves, we are shown how George blames Lennie for making his life difficult. The source of George's irritation seems to be the burden of responsibility he has for Lennie. George fantasizes about what life would be like on his own: *"I could get along so easy and so nice if I didn't have you on my tail. I could live so easy and maybe have a girl."*

They prepare for dinner, and much to George's annoyance, Lennie retrieves the dead mouse instead of collecting firewood. This time George explains as if to a child that dead mice make bad pets. For the benefit of the reader, he also makes it known that this is not the first mouse that Lennie has adopted. Unfortunately, and in a warning of events to come later in the story, we also learn that this gentle giant of a man always kills his pet mice accidentally because he is unaware of his own great strength. Lennie, not realizing that George is in no mood to talk about the rabbits, mentions them again. As darkness descends George finally explodes with frustration when Lennie states for a second time that he likes ketchup with his beans, a luxury they do not have. George asserts his desire for freedom in a more realistic and detailed way than he did previously, saying that he could take the money he earns each month, and do whatever he likes, which includes drinking, womanizing, and gambling. ✪ Keeping the ending in mind, why is this ironic?

George ends his explosion by giving us information about Lennie innocently clutching at the dress of an increasingly distressed girl, *to pet it like it was a mouse.* Not surprisingly, this incident put them on the run and on the road.

A subdued George and an affectionate Lennie, eager to appease his friend discuss the possibility of parting company. In a simple but dignified way Lennie asserts himself and also shows that he has needs and desires that are not being met in their relationship by saying that he could keep mice if he was on his own.

Lennie, George, and the dream

Lennie's bid for independence acts as a trigger to George to show remorse because he thinks he has been mean to Lennie. He promises him a puppy to make amends. For a brief moment, Lennie is a more equal partner in the relationship and he is clever enough in emotional territory to use George's guilt to get him to tell the story of the lives they wish they had – a story he has heard many times before.

George explains that ranch hands are *the loneliest guys in the world*, who waste their money and have nothing to look forward to, but that for them it will be different. They won't be *blowin' in our jack* (spending savings), but will have a smallholding and *live off the fatta the lan'*. At last we hear more about the fantasy rabbits that Lennie is so anxious to care for.

Lennie to return if there's trouble

The tension between the two melts away, and, as they eat, they are again friendly. Lennie even shows signs of remembering important things. Steinbeck makes George use this as a way to make his friend remember something else – that if Lennie gets into trouble he is to return and hide in the brush until George comes for him. For the first time, we are introduced to the main effective threat that George uses as a control over Lennie's behavior – that if he gets into trouble, he won't get to tend the rabbits.

Test yourself

? Who is Aunt Clara?
? Describe the duo's dream for the future in your own words.
? What reasons do you think George has to be frustrated with Lennie?

now give yourself a treat before you settle into the bunkhouse

Scene 2

◆ George and Lennie settle into the bunkhouse and hear about the other ranch hands.
◆ George and Lennie meet the boss.
◆ They also meet Curley.
◆ George tells Lennie to avoid Curley, and reminds him where to hide if he gets into trouble.
◆ Curley's wife visits the bunkhouse. Lennie is warned to avoid her too.
◆ Slim and Carlson introduced. Slim's dog has puppies, and Lennie wants one.

George and Lennie settle into the bunkhouse

By introducing the two main characters in the first scene and presenting their relationship, Steinbeck wins our loyalty to them and makes us curious to know what happens to them. The scene shifts and we have been manipulated into looking at life on the ranch from their point of view.

It is a sunny morning, full of the promise that accompanies bright weather. Steinbeck begins with a description of the bunkhouse, a dormitory for eight people, with bedding made of thick canvas covers called *burlap ticking*. The bunkhouse is quite basic. Shelving for the few personal belongings each temporary resident owns consists of a box for packing apples. Toiletries are the main effects to be found on the shelves, but *those Western magazines ranch-men love to read and scoff at and secretly believe* can be found there too. ❂ What does this sentence imply about the dreams and fantasies of hard-working ranchmen?

The bunkhouse has makeshift seating consisting of more boxes. Old Candy the cleaner known as a swamper, who is not named at this stage, warns the newcomers that the boss is angry that they are late. They see a can of insecticide and learn from the old man that cockroaches and lice, referred to as *pants rabbits* and *greybacks* are no strangers to these accommodations. Even so, some ranchers take care with their personal hygiene. One, a blacksmith named Whitey, was especially particular. His name might be a reference to an obsession with cleanliness or Steinbeck's way of laying foundations for the racial discrimination from which Crooks, a African-American man and stable buck, or stable boy, will suffer later in the story. Steinbeck is probably also making a point about the self-respect itinerant workers manage to retain, despite the difficult circumstances under which they live.

George and Lennie meet the boss

In preparation for meeting the boss, we hear a little about him through Candy's eyes. His first observation is that the boss regularly takes his anger out on Crooks who is not named at this stage either, although we hear that he has a crooked back from a horse's kick. Candy says: *"Ya see the stable buck's a nigger."*

The comment reveals the attitude that being African-American is a reason in itself to be picked on, regardless of whether the person has done anything to deserve it. Not only is Crooks African-American and the boss white, but Crooks is a lowly worker and the boss has all the power. The unequal relationship between the boss and Crooks is thus established.

In his favor, the boss has been generous with whiskey for the workers at Christmas time. The gathering even allowed *Crooks* to join them on that occasion, but they also have the same discriminatory attitudes as the boss because they are white. This is demonstrated by the account of the fight in which Crooks is picked on. He was considered fair game because he was of his race, but ironically, in an attempt to level the odds, his opponent is not allowed to use his feet in the fight to compensate for Crooks' deformed back. ✪ Who wins this fight? Do you believe the reason why?

As the *fat-legged* boss begins to ask questions, George reminds Lennie with a scowl that he must keep quiet, and Lennie's nod suggests that he understands. All too quickly Lennie forgets, however. He is put under pressure from the boss to speak for himself, because, not surprisingly, the boss suspects that George is exploiting Lennie. ✪ What does the boss say and do to confirm this?

The boss's probing questions and lingering stare of suspicion provide a further cloud over the sunny morning. George is all too aware of the impression they have made, and Lennie's forgetfulness plunges him into a *morosely silent* mood. His despair is deepening. George owns up to his lie that Lennie had been kicked in the head as a child. It is as if a reason for Lennie's simpleness makes it more acceptable. He probably thought of it because of the recent talk of Crooks' injury, which had been the fault of a horse, but it cleverly has the effect of providing something in common between two of the most bullied characters in the novel.

What can you remember?

? What two items of the boss's clothing prove he was not a laborer? Draw a picture to help you remember.
? What animal is Lennie compared to when he meets the boss? Why is this?

George and Lennie meet Curley

Candy reenters the bunkhouse with his old dog and reassures a nervous George that he has not been listening to their private conversation. He is followed by Curley, the boss's son. The glove that Curley wears is a work glove, but like his father he also wears high-heeled boots to demonstrate that he is no laborer. Curley, who enjoys his position of power as the boss's son, likes to intimidate the workers. He constantly stirs up trouble, even trying to provoke a gentle giant like Lennie.

In an attempt to explain Curley's aggressive behavior, Candy, a receptacle of gossip and rumor says that because he is small, Curley is *"alla time picking scraps with big guys."* He also points out the unfairness of the situation in which Curley is always the winner – if he wins a fight against a big man he is seen as tough; if he loses, people will say the big man had an unfair advantage.

Candy, still unnamed, goes on to say that Curley's behavior has been worse since he recently married a woman who is already trying to flirt with the more senior workers, Slim and Carlson.

George gives important instructions

As Candy leaves the dark bunkhouse to enter the brilliant sunshine, George plays solitaire, a card game for one person associated with the lonely. He expresses his dislike of Curley to Lennie and warns him what may happen. He impresses upon Lennie the importance of keeping away from Curley and reminds him to return to the place where they camped the previous evening if he gets into trouble. We are already aware that if anyone picks a fight it will be Curley, and that whatever happens, Lennie will probably not have any power or ability to influence the situation. Although he does win "round one" later in the bunkhouse, Lennie cannot defeat so formidable, if cowardly, an opponent in the long term.

Curley's wife visits the bunkhouse

In another warning of what is to come and how Curley's wife will be the cause of permanent darkness to Lennie, when she makes her first appearance: *the rectangle of sunshine in the doorway was cut off.* (For a note on Steinbeck's use of light, see Language, Style, and Structure, p. 31.) As if bearing out Candy's dismissal of her as *a tart*, Steinbeck presents her as one. No mention is made of her features, and even her ringlets are referred to unflatteringly, as resembling sausages.

She unconvincingly states that she is looking for her husband as she thrusts herself forward invitingly. The simple Lennie's eyes *moved down over her body in fascination*, and again we sense trouble, particularly as she is the wife of the boss's son. ✪ Why do you think she is *apprehensive* when Slim tells her he just saw Curley go into the house?

George instantly recognizes the trouble there might be if Lennie so much as speaks to Curley's wife. He issues yet another warning to Lennie to keep away from such *jail bait*. He is already burdened by having so much to remember, but as he showed during the previous evening, Lennie is not so simple when it comes to picking up on atmospheres and perhaps sensing his own destiny. He voices what we are thinking when he says: *This ain't no good place, I wanna get outa here ... It's mean here.* Ironically, it is George who keeps them there in his anxiety to plan ahead and accrue some savings.

Slim and Carlson introduced

Slim is responsible for operating the rope that connects the leading horse with the brake of the vehicle. He is described with detailed praise. At last, we think, a fair man. Perhaps things are not so bad after all. Steinbeck creates a more relaxed atmosphere in the bunkhouse as George and Slim become acquainted with each other. Carlson, *a powerful, big-stomached man*, also enters the bunkhouse and seems accepting, rather than antagonistic, toward the newcomers.

The conversation shifts to Slim's dog and her new puppies. In the first time that Candy is named, Carlson suggests that the old man's dog should be put down and that Slim could give him one of the puppies. Lennie, quicker in all matters concerning animals, does not need to tell George he wants a puppy too. George knows and promises to ask for him.

The scene closes with the newlywed, Curley, turning up at the bunkhouse in search of his wife. This time the focus of his attention is George.

Try a test

? What is Curley's wife wearing when she first appears in the bunkhouse? Why do you think Steinbeck chooses to describe her in this way?

? Think about Steinbeck's description of Slim and what this says about him. Draw or note down an image to sum up his skills.

? When the men first leave the bunkhouse to go to supper, Carlson *stepped back to let Slim precede him.* Why?

now take a break and brace yourself for a sad incident

Scene 3

◆ George confides in Slim.
◆ Carlson persuades Candy that his old dog must die.
◆ The men in the bunkhouse talk about women.
◆ George, Lennie, and Candy make plans to buy a smallholding.
◆ Curley picks a fight with Lennie.
◆ Curley is sent to the doctor.

George confides in Slim

A reference to the brightness outdoors and the dusk inside the bunkhouse opens the scene. These are probably symbols of the troubled atmosphere inside and the freedom beyond. Slim acknowledges Lennie's great strength and ability to work, and George thanks Slim for giving Lennie a puppy from which he is becoming inseparable. The other workers play a game outside.

George opens up to Slim about his relationship with Lennie. His fondness for Lennie shows in the way that he speaks of the two of them as companions rather than as one dependent on the other. ✪ What does this say about who is dependent on whom?

In what Steinbeck describes as a *tone of confession*, George, pleased to talk to someone about his problems with Lennie, tells the story of how Lennie nearly drowned, just as four of Slim's helpless puppies had to be drowned. So great was Lennie's loyalty to George that he did as he was told, jumped in the river, but couldn't swim. George again begins playing solitaire, a pastime that seems to express the part of him that wants to be alone, and to foreshadow the time when he will be.

As the conversation becomes more confidential, we are reminded of the incident in Weed. George compares the way Lennie held onto the girl's dress to the way he cannot leave the puppies alone now. To reinforce the point, Steinbeck makes Lennie comes back to the bunkhouse hiding his puppy. George reminds Lennie and the reader that it is too small to leave its mother, and in a portent of doom, adds: *"You'll kill him, the first thing you know."*

Candy's dog must die

The men return to the bunkhouse in the darkness of night, after playing horseshoes, a game Crooks has been allowed to participate in and excels in. ✪ Why do you think Steinbeck mentions this when we have not yet been introduced to him?

Carlson complains about Candy's old, nameless dog smelling bad, and offers to shoot him. The old man resists, but Carlson is determined and even Slim agrees that the time for the dog to die has come. Whit, the young laborer, tries to distract the group with a Western magazine that includes a letter from a former worker, but Carlson persists. Eventually he leads the dog *out into the darkness* of the night and to its death.

Steinbeck creates a tense atmosphere in the bunkhouse as the men wait to hear the shot. Their silence reveals a concern and humanity that is rarely seen on the ranch. They try to fill the silence that *came out of the night and invaded the room*, with card games and conversation, but silence returns and is referred to several more times before the shot is heard.

At last we meet Crooks, who has prepared some tar to treat a mule's foot. In contrast with the old dog that has just been shot, and drawing the similarity between Candy and Lennie who both display sentimentality over their dogs, he reminds us that Lennie cannot leave the pups alone, and they are too young to be played with.

The men talk about women

As Whit reminds us of Curley's wife's flirting, George again plays solitaire. He predicts that she is ... *gonna make a mess. They're gonna be a bad mess about her.* It seems more than likely that he is right and that she could land a man in jail.

As a sign that George is becoming accepted by the group, Whit invites him to go with them to town to visit a brothel. His description of the two possible places to which they might go is enthusiastic. This has the effect of emphasizing how lonely and separated from family life migrant workers are.

Carlson cleans his gun after shooting the dog, and Candy remains silent. Curley makes no secret of his suspicion that his wife, whom he cannot find, is with Slim in the barn. One by one, the men leave the bunkhouse in anticipation of enjoying the confrontation. A subdued Lennie is questioned by George who thinks he may have seen Curley's wife, but Lennie assures him that his manner is due to worry that George will think he has done wrong by playing with and petting the puppies too much.

Think this through

? When George talks confidentially to Slim, he owns up to how he used to regard knowing Lennie as a boost to his image. What does he say exactly?
? What makes the shooting of Candy's old dog inevitable?
? What do you think of the attitude of the workers to women?

now treat yourself to a break before you share a dream

George, Lennie, and Candy make plans

Tired of all the undercurrents on the ranch, Lennie asks George when they can *get that little place an' live on the fatta the lan' – an' rabbits*. For the first time since his dog has been shot, Candy stirs. George, his voice *growing warmer*, forgets to play solitaire as he describes the *little place we can get cheap*. It is significant that this time when the dream is repeated, it concerns an actual place, and George describes it in some detail. The need to settle down and take pride in his work is revealed when he says they would *know what come of our plantin'*, and there would be no danger of being sacked or canned.

Lennie, who, as usual, cannot hear enough about rabbits, shows the only sign of intentional violence in the whole story at this point. Even now it is directed at *the future cats which might dare to disturb the future rabbits*. As the dream takes on a more realistic quality, both men engrossed in the fantasy, Candy joins in with questions of a practical and financial nature.

Candy's money, and his offer to make a will in their favor, increases the sense of the dream becoming reality. The idea that *they had never really believed in was coming true*. George decides to put the plan into action in only one month's time and resolves to send some money to secure the place. George tells the others not to tell anyone about the plan.

Candy expresses his regret that he didn't shoot his dog himself. This acts almost as advice to George later on when he faces a difficult decision about Lennie.

Curley picks a fight with Lennie

The mood created by discussing the dream is abruptly broken up by the return of the other men to the bunkhouse. Slim has resisted Curley's accusations about him and his wife, and Curley apologizes. Carlson accuses him of cowardice, and Candy joins in baiting Curley.

It is Lennie, however, the big guy who won't be able to win, who Curley picks on. Lennie shows no sign of violence despite the injuries that Curley is inflicting on him. Only when George

repeats the command to *get 'im* does Lennie act. Even then, all
he does, and all he needs to do, is grab Curley's fist as it
comes toward him to bring the fight to a swift end. Just as he
would not let go of the red dress in Weed for fright, so he
hangs on to Curley's severely damaged fist. ✪ Why do you
think Steinbeck makes Curley pick on Lennie immediately after
the scene in which the dream may become reality?

Curley is sent to the doctor

Slim and Carlson organize medical treatment for Curley. In
response to George's concern that they might get the sack for
what has happened to the boss's son, Slim thinks quickly and
makes Curley promise not to tell anyone. In return for his
silence, he will not then be made a laughingstock.

The scene closes with further acknowledgments of Lennie's
strength and reassurances that the incident had not been his fault.
Most important of all, to Lennie, he still gets to tend the rabbits.

Test yourself

?   Why does George think the trio might be able to buy
      the place cheap?

?   What are Candy's reasons for wanting to join them?
      Make a mini Mind Map.

?   What reason does Slim tell Curley to give for his
      broken hand?

you might want a break before you join Crooks

Scene 4

◆ Lennie visits Crooks.
◆ Crooks taunts Lennie about George leaving him.
◆ Candy joins Crooks and Lennie. They discuss the future farm.
◆ Curley's wife also visits Crooks.

Lennie visits Crooks

The scene shifts to Crooks' room next to the barn. It is full of horse equipment under repair, and we learn that Crooks is able to leave his personal possessions lying around, free from the prying eyes of the communal bunkhouse. He has more possessions than the other workers because a stable buck's job is more permanent.

CROOKS HAS MIXED FEELINGS

As Crooks treats his old injury with a lotion, Lennie, looking for company, on a lonely Saturday night when all the others are in town, appears in the doorway. At first he is not welcomed by the bitter and resentful Crooks, who is usually segregated from the whites on the ranch. Out of pride, Crooks asserts his right to privacy in his own room.

Ironically, Crooks is desperately lonely, and so he eventually invites Lennie in to sit down. Lennie has characteristically forgotten that he is not to talk about the plan for the future, because the rabbits are so much on his mind. He doesn't really listen to Crooks, who talks of his childhood and the roots of his isolation. Perhaps to emphasize their loneliness, Steinbeck stops his characters from listening to each other. He does this again several times later. ✪ Can you find another example?

Crooks taunts Lennie

Out of envy because he has a companion, Crooks taunts Lennie with the idea that George may desert him. Although Lennie is sure that George will come back, Crooks upsets him with the suggestion that George may be hurt, a prospect that almost causes Lennie to become violent. By his moving speech, Crooks hopes Lennie will understand how lonely it is for him not to be allowed into the bunkhouse to play cards and have company, but all Lennie can think about is where George might be.

Crooks doubts that he understands things properly, or sees the same things as other people, because, he has no companion to discuss things with. This is ironic because he soon reveals that he is a realist who is well aware of the dreams of ranchers with *a little piece of land* in mind, and how these men fail to realize their plans. He perceives the social inequalities and the economic difficulties facing them.

Candy, Crooks, and Lennie discuss the future

Crooks' talk of the ranch where he spent his childhood, and the mention of alfalfa makes Lennie forget about George. Candy turns up at Crooks' room, and because he is so unaccustomed to visitors, Crooks cannot *conceal his pleasure with anger*. They talk about the rabbits and the proposed piece of land because Candy has forgotten his vow of silence too. Crooks again dismisses their plan as just a dream until he hears they have both the money and an actual place in mind. He almost believes it might really happen, and he asks to be included in the plan.

Curley's wife also visits Crooks

Curley's wife joins the gathering on the pretext of looking for Curley, who has gone carousing in town, as she well knows. She astutely observes that "the weak ones" have been left behind – Crooks, because he is African-American, Lennie, because he is slow, and Candy because he is old and disabled.

Despite their differences, however, she has much in common with them. They are all outsiders, they are all left at the ranch on a Saturday night, they lead lonely lives, and they all have dreams. Hers, which we hear of for the first time is that she ... *could have went with shows. Not jus' one, neither. An' a guy tol' me he could put me in pitchers.*

As she probes for the truth about the injury to Curley's fist, she complains that the men won't talk to her when in pairs or more and that she has nothing to do on a Saturday night, the traditional night for going out and having fun, from which all of these characters are excluded. ✪ What does she say to reveal her opinion of her husband?

Tired and angry at her insults, and boosted by increased self-respect and a new interest in life, Candy explodes and tells her boldly about their plan. She echoes Crooks' earlier disbelief, scoffs at it, and guesses the truth about Lennie's involvement in Curley's injury, adding that she may get some rabbits herself if it will please Lennie.

In a display of his meager rights, Crooks tries to make her leave. She responds by threatening to exercise what little power she has by getting Crooks hanged if he tells on her for leaving the house. This has the effect of bringing them all back to reality about their actual situation, just as the revellers return from town.

Crooks asks Lennie and Candy to leave, and George is angry that the plan has been revealed. The spell broken, Crooks tells Candy to forget his request to join the prospective landowners, and as the scene opened, tends his bad back alone in his room.

A few questions for you to think about

?   According to Crooks, what happens when a person gets lonely?

?   What agreement do Lennie and Candy forget they have made when they visit Crooks? Why is the agreement important?

?   How does Steinbeck describe the effect Curley's wife has on Crooks?

find out how Lennie gets into trouble — after a break

Scene 5

◆ Lennie has killed his puppy.
◆ Curley's wife tells her story.
◆ Lennie kills Curley's wife.
◆ Candy and George discover the body.
◆ The news comes out.

Lennie has killed his puppy

It is Sunday afternoon and the workers are relaxing. Most of the men are playing horseshoes outside, but Lennie is alone in the barn. He talks to his dead puppy, another victim of the big man's enormous strength that he has again failed to control.

His main concern is that he won't get to tend the rabbits on the future land. He wonders how bad his action is.

Curley's wife tells her story

Curley's wife, heavily made up, enters the barn and tells Lennie she wants to talk to him because she gets *awful lonely.*
He remembers that he has been warned not to talk to her and tells her so. Prophetically he says: *"George says you'll get us in a mess."*

She tells Lennie her dream of being in the movies, and how she married Curley out of desperation when her hopes were dashed. As they did in Crooks' room, this pair of misfits pursue their own thoughts of films and rabbits rather than taking an interest in each other's hopes and dreams.

Curley's wife hopes to impress Lennie with her story and she confesses to him that she doesn't like her husband. ❂ From her account of how she almost became an actress, how real do you think the opportunity was?

Lennie kills Curley's wife

As Lennie mentions the imaginary smallholding and the imaginary rabbits, the two sit closer together, and talk about petting *nice things.* Then, in an echo of the past and in the realization of George's worst fears, Curley's wife invites Lennie to touch her hair.

Her appeals to him to be careful not to mess up her hair and his worry that George will be angry when she yells combine to make Lennie hang on tightly, as he did with the girl's dress in Weed and later with Curley's fist. Lennie, unaware as ever of his own great strength, breaks her neck.

Soon he begins to understand the seriousness of what he has done and says: *"I shouldn't have did that. George'll be mad."* Then he remembers George's instruction about returning to the campsite they used on their way to the ranch and to hide and wait in the brush if he gets into trouble. Lennie is still concerned that the dead puppy should not be discovered, and as he did with the mouse in the opening scene, takes it with him.

Candy and George discover the body

As if the soul of Curley's wife leaves her body for a better life in death, so *the sun streaks were high on the wall by now.* She is at peace at last. As if in disbelief, the animals in the barn are quiet as the *moment settled and hovered and remained for much more than a moment.* By the time Candy discovers the body, the animals are restless: *The horses stamped and snorted, and they chewed the straw of their bedding and they clashed the chains of their halters.*

Candy gets George, and the two wonder what to do. George concludes that the others will have to be told and that Lennie will have to be jailed or he will starve on his own. It is a touching moment in the story because it makes it clear that George knows the killing had been an accident, and he is more concerned with Lennie's welfare than his punishment.

Candy reminds George that Curley, already thirsty for revenge on Lennie for his fist, will want to kill him, and the pair acknowledges that their dream is over. George considers the life ahead of him, working and partying. Candy agrees to let George appear to know only as the others find out to prevent any suggestion of conspiracy with Lennie. Candy also expresses his sorrow that his dreams have been shattered.

The news comes out

Just as the animals were quiet immediately after the killing, the men who come in from outdoors are also subdued and dazed for a moment. Curley then reacts in rage and vows to shoot Lennie, with Carlson a willing accomplice. Slim and George discuss locking Lennie up if they can stop Curley from getting to him first, and Slim voices the opinion that jailing Lennie would be cruel.

Carlson thinks Lennie has stolen his gun, but we know he did not. This reveals why George went to the bunkhouse before pretending the murder is news; he has already come to terms with the fate that Lennie must meet and has taken the gun himself. Ironically, the ranch hands assume Lennie, not George, has taken Carlson's gun. This makes Lennie's death certain as they believe he is armed. George's appeals to Curley not to shoot Lennie fall on deaf ears. Curley, showing more anger than grief, repeats his determination to kill Lennie himself. He shows no sign of grief for his wife and insists on George going with them to establish his innocence. Darkness descends on Candy and the barn.

Test your memory

?   How do the animals in the barn react to the death of Curley's wife?

?   Why do you think George is so sure that Curley's wife's death is an accident?

?   What make is Carlson's gun?

?   Make a Mind Map showing the men's different reactions to the death of Curley's wife.

take a break to prepare for a tragic conclusion

Scene 6

◆ Lennie has hallucinations.
◆ George and Lennie say good-bye.
◆ George shoots Lennie.

Lennie has hallucinations

As the story began, so it ends. The animal kingdom at the campsite by the river is playing out the cycle of hunter and prey. ✪ How does this differ from the description of the same scene in the opening pages? In a foreshadowing of what is to come, the sun, used as a symbol of life, has left the valley for the tops of the mountains, symbols of the afterlife.

Lennie finds the place and sits to wait for George. In a pathetic and unknowing prediction of his own fate, he says: *"George gonna wish he was alone an' not have me botherin' him ... If George don't want me ... I'll go away."* As if in a deteriorating state of mind brought on by the guilt he feels for letting George down, rather than for what he has done, he begins to see things.

First, a vision of Aunt Clara chides him for being so much trouble to George. She speaks in Lennie's voice, however, because she is a manifestation of his own thoughts and disgust with himself.

The idea that he won't get to *tend no rabbits now* is enough to create a picture of a rabbit. Again, the apparition speaks with Lennie's voice, and it is telling him that he would probably forget to feed the rabbits anyway. In a continuation of the theme of loneliness, the rabbit adds of George: *"He gonna leave ya all alone."*

George and Lennie say good-bye

As the two friends share in their last conversation, and the sound of the ranchers advances, the sun retreats further up the mountains, taking hope with it. In an attempt to invite the punishment from George that he expects, but isn't given, Lennie makes George tell him how he would like to be on his own. This has a saddening effect on the reader, who, unlike Lennie, knows he is recounting his own sad fate as just another ranch hand with broken dreams.

When Lennie draws a statement from George that he wants them to stick together, Lennie makes his friend tell the story of how they will live off *the fatta the lan'*. Lennie's childlike simplicity in a cruel world, the threat of the ranchers nearing, George's new loneliness, and the painful telling of a story once bright with hope and now dashed in pieces, again increases the sense of sadness and sympathy for the two.

As George instructs Lennie to remove his hat, and the shadow in the valley deepens, we know the dreaded moment is coming closer. As George plucks up courage, they continue talking. Although Lennie's back is turned and he is unaware of George's intention, the words he uses to urge George to tell the story have the effect of sounding like he is helping George to get ready to kill him. As the ranchers are close by he says: *"Go on,"* *"When we gonna do it?"* and *"Let's do it now,"* as if he is talking about pulling the trigger rather than realizing a dream. George finally reassures Lennie of the dream future that is really the kind of heaven he hopes his friend will find.

George shoots Lennie

Lennie dies, unaware of what is happening to him, but happy in George's reassurances for their future. George stares at his hand in disbelief, and agrees with Carlson's statement that Lennie had stolen the gun and that George had gotten it from him. No one but George knows that he took it, because unlike Candy, who regretted not shooting his own dog himself, George has taken responsibility. He has saved Lennie from Curley, as if putting a dog out of its misery in the kindest way possible. Lennie dies with dignity. It is perhaps the final irony that George's brave act probably looks to the other ranch hands as if he took the coward's way out by shooting Lennie in the back.

George's only comfort as the story closes is the friendship of Slim. Curley and Carlson have so little compassion that they are genuinely surprised to witness the sadness of George and Slim. The last comment from Carlson ends the story on a note of harsh reality about the world.

What do you think?

? Look at the image of the water snake in the first and last scenes. How effective is the image and do you think it serves a purpose in developing the story?

? Do you agree with Lennie's imaginary rabbit when it says to him: *"You ain't fit to lick the boots of no rabbit"*?

? Do you think anyone other than George would have been able to kill Lennie without Lennie knowing it was going to happen? Give reasons for your answer.

? Briefly tell the story of each scene next to the pictures on page 62.

Scene 1

Scene 2

Scene 3

Scene 4

Scene 5

Scene 6

TOPICS FOR DISCUSSION AND BRAINSTORMING

One of the best ways to review is with one or more friends. Even if you're with someone who hardly knows the text you're studying, you'll find that having to explain things to your friend will help you to organize your own thoughts and memorize key points. If you're with someone who has studied the text, you'll find that the things you can't remember are different from the things your friend can't remember, so you'll be able to help each other.

Discussion will also help you to develop interesting new ideas that perhaps neither of you would have had alone. Use a **brainstorming** approach to tackle any of the topics listed below. Allow yourself to share whatever ideas come into your head – however meaningless they seem. This will get you thinking creatively.

Whether alone or with a friend, use Mind Mapping (see p. viii) to help you brainstorm and organize your ideas. If you are with a friend, use a large sheet of paper and thick colored pens.

Any of the topics below could appear on an exam, but even if you think you've found one on your actual exam, be sure to read the question carefully and answer the precise question given.

Background

1 How did the Depression affect the lives of ordinary Americans in the 1930s?
2 Which of the following had been introduced in America by the time *Of Mice and Men* was written?

- beer cans
- nylon stockings
- the instant camera
- the launderette
- sliced bread
- fluorescent lighting
- the TV dinner
- microwave ovens
- FM radio

(You can check your answers by looking back to p. xiv.)

3 How are Steinbeck's life and beliefs reflected in *Of Mice and Men?*

Summary

Look at the summary list of key points below. Can you number them from one to ten in the right order?

- Lennie kills Curley's wife.
- Lennie and Candy visit Crooks.
- Curley picks a fight with Lennie.
- Lennie kills his puppy.
- George warns Lennie to keep away from Curley and his wife.
- George shoots Lennie.
- George and Lennie are on their way to new jobs.
- Carlson shoots Candy's old dog.
- Lennie's pet mouse is dead.
- Candy joins in the plan to buy a smallholding.

Character

1 Write two short **curriculum vitaes** (life histories) for George and Lennie as if they were applying for a job. Remember to include age, address, educational history and achievements, work experience, and interests.

2 Who is being described in the following extracts? Try to remember before you look them up:

(a) *A powerful, big-stomached man.*

(b) *A young labouring man came in. His sloping shoulders were bent forward and he walked heavily on his heels, as though he carried the invisible grain bag.*

(c) *... a tall stoop-shouldered old man came in.*

3 Describe these characters in your own words:

(a) Curley.

(b) Curley's wife.

(c) Slim.

4 Who said the following, in what context, and what does the statement mean? (If you can't remember, look them up!)

(a) *"OK, Machine. I'll talk to you later. I like machines."*

(b) *"You ain't fit to lick the boots of no rabbit."*

(c) *"Why do you got to get killed? You ain't so little as mice."*

5 Do you feel sympathy for any of the characters in *Of Mice and Men*? If so, which ones and why?

6 Find an incident or conversation in the text to support the following statements:

(a) George believes he would be happier without Lennie.

(b) Curley's wife uses excuses to visit men.

(c) Crooks had a happy childhood.

Language

1 Why did Steinbeck use the title *Of Mice and Men*?

2 Find the words in the text that mean the same as the following statements. What do you notice about the difference between each one of these and the one it corresponds to in the book?

(a) "You might be a good boxer, but you're a coward. If you attack me, I'll defend myself."

(b) "They're all playing games, it's early, and I need someone to talk to."

(c) "Everyone dreams of owning a smallholding, but nobody actually does it."

3 Why doesn't Steinbeck give Curley's wife a name?

4 What effect does the use of nicknames have on the way the characters are defined?

5 Comment on Steinbeck's use of imagery in *Of Mice and Men*.

6 Comment on Steinbeck's use of irony in *Of Mice and Men*.

7 Why does Steinbeck compare Lennie to large animals such as bears and bulls? How far do such descriptions prepare the reader for events that take place in the book?

8 Do you think the story would end differently if Curley was away from the ranch when his wife's death is discovered?

Themes

1 Jot down the names of the characters who dream of the following, and say why their dreams are not achieved (there may be more than one for each):

(a) Owning land.

(b) Acting in the movies.

(c) Tending rabbits.

(d) Making friends and being treated fairly.

2 Curley's wife is treated badly by the men. Do you agree?
3 What happens to ranch people when they get lonely? What can they do about it?
4 Comment on the friendship between George and Lennie.

Style and structure

1 What contributions do Candy's and Slim's dogs make to the development of the story?
2 How believable is the story?
3 How important is location, or the setting, in the book?
4 Some people think that Lennie's hallucinations in the final scene are out of place and a weak part of the novel. Do you agree or disagree? Why?
5 What is the difference between plot and theme? Think of examples from *Of Mice and Men* to illustrate the difference.
6 Why do you think Steinbeck chose not to use chapters?
7 What is the climax or most significant event in each of the six sections?
8 Which part of the book do you find easiest to understand? Why?
9 Which part is most difficult? What can you do to improve your understanding?

HOW TO GET AN "A" IN ENGLISH LITERATURE

In all your study, in coursework, and in exams, be aware of the following:

- **Characterization** – the characters and what we know about them (what they say and do, how the author describes them), their relationships, and how they develop.
- **Plot and structure** – what happens and how the plot is organized into parts or episodes.
- **Setting and atmosphere** – the changing scene and how it reflects the story (for example, a rugged landscape and storm reflecting a character's emotional difficulties).
- **Style and language** – the author's choice of words and literary devices such as imagery and how these reflect the mood.
- **Viewpoint** – how the story is told (for example, through an imaginary narrator, or in the third person but through the eyes of one character – "She was furious – how dare he!").
- **Social and historical context** – influences on the author (see Background in this guide).

Develop your ability to:

- Relate **detail** to **broader content, meaning, and style**.
- Show understanding of the author's **intentions, technique, and meaning** (brief and appropriate comparisons with other works by the same author will earn credit.
- Give **personal response and interpretation**, backed up by **examples** and short **quotations**.
- **Evaluate** the author's achievement (how completely does the author succeed and why?)

THE EXAM ESSAY

Planning

A literary essay of about 250 to 400 words on a theme from *Of Mice and Men* will challenge your skills as an essay writer. It is worth taking some time to plan your essay carefully. An excellent way to do this is in the three stages below:

1 Make a **Mind Map** of your ideas on the theme suggested. Brainstorm and write down any ideas that pop into your head.
2 Taking ideas from your Mind Map, **organize** them into an outline choosing a logical sequence of information. Choose significant details and quotations to support your main thesis.
3 Be sure you have both a strong **opening paragraph** stating your main idea and giving the title and author of the literary work you will be discussing, and a **conclusion** that sums up your main points.

Writing and Editing

Write your essay carefully, allowing at least five minutes at the end to check for errors of fact as well as for correct spelling, grammar, and punctuation.

REMEMBER!

Stick to the thesis you are trying to support and avoid unnecessary plot summary. Always support your ideas with relevant details and quotations from the text.

Model Answer and Plan

The next (and final) chapter consists of a model essay on a theme from *Of Mice and Men* followed by a Mind Map and an essay plan used to write it. Use these to get an idea of how an essay about *Of Mice and Men* might be organized and how to break up your information into a logical sequence of paragraphs.

Before reading the answer, you might like to do a plan of your own, then compare it with the example. The numbered points with comments at the end show why it's a good answer.

QUESTION

"Lennie's worst enemy is his own strength." How far do you agree with this statement?

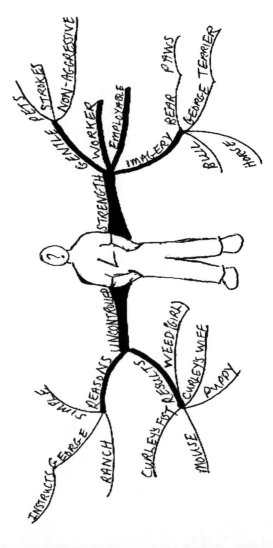

PLAN

1 Lennie is certainly strong (examples/imagery).
2 Part of Lennie's strength plays in development of story.
3 Strength is an advantage too (getting work/self-defense).
4 Lack of control over strength.
  (a) brutality not intentional (except imaginary cats).
  (b) hostile world/ranch conditions.
  (c) problem of not letting go (examples).
5 Conclusion. Real problem lack of control over strength.

ESSAY

Lennie Small is a gentle giant who possesses an almost superhuman strength that ultimately leads to tragedy. We first read about Lennie's great strength in the opening scene when he has killed, probably by accident, the pet mouse he has in his pocket. We learn that it is not the first time Lennie has killed pets. During the same scene, Steinbeck compares him to a bear and a horse, both strong animals. This imagery of Lennie as an animal continues. He is also compared to a terrier, indicating that he is a faithful and loyal companion to George.

Steinbeck makes his characters pick up the animal references too. When George tells the boss that Lennie is: "Strong as a bull," Lennie repeats the statement. The repetition has the effect of again giving the reader clues that Lennie's strength will be significant to the development of the story. Steinbeck fully develops the animal comparison at the end by drawing a parallel between Candy and his no longer useful old dog, and George as the master of the doglike Lennie, who can no longer be useful after he has accidentally killed Curley's wife.

All the other characters witness Lennie's strength sooner or later. George mentions it frequently, and Slim says: "... I never seen such a worker. He damn near killed his partner buckin' barley. There ain't nobody can keep up with him. God Almighty, I never seen such a strong guy."

Demonstrations of Lennie's strength continue with details of the incident in Weed when Lennie is accused of assaulting a girl, which we do not witness, the mangling of Curley's fist, and the accidental killing of both the puppy and Curley's wife.

There are times when Lennie's strength is a positive

advantage, however, and, if harnessed appropriately, which George attempts to do as much as he can, it is a virtue. As long as Lennie keeps quiet at interviews and lets George do the talking, he makes an excellent impression as a worker and probably contributes greatly to ensuring that the pair continue to find work during a period of very high unemployment during the Great Depression. He is also able to defend himself, which George calls upon him to do when Curley attacks him for no real reason. Sadly, this could be a useful attribute to have in places where many unhappy men are cooped up together with few opportunities to take a break from each other.

The problem of Lennie's strength, therefore, is his lack of ability to control it, and it is important not to overlook that Lennie's brutal actions are never intentional. As Slim notices: "He ain't mean. I can see Lennie ain't a bit mean." And as Lennie says to George: "I don't want no trouble...Don't let him sock me, George."

Lennie's endearing qualities and lack of aggression are never better demonstrated than when George tells Lennie that should Curley try to fight him, he should "let 'im have it," and Lennie replies: 'Let 'im have what, George?' If Lennie had Curley's mean temperament, he really would be dangerous. Only when the dream of living off the fat of the land seems realizable does Lennie show any signs of aggression. Even then, the objects of his anger are "imaginary cats" that could threaten "imaginary rabbits."

Lennie's lack of control over his own strength would probably be limited to the harm he innocently inflicts on his pets if he lived and worked in more sympathetic surroundings, but the ranch is a hostile place, full of desperate characters, where inequalities of power and prosperity are very apparent and exploited. If Curley and his father, the boss, were kinder and if Curley treated his wife with the respect he should have shown toward her, the tragic conclusion would not have occurred.

Against this background, Lennie likes to touch and pet soft things, and each of the three times when it really matters he becomes frightened and won't let go. At Weed he touches a girl's dress, and she misunderstands his simple intentions. When Curley bullies him he crushes his fist, instead of warning Curley off with less pressure because he gets scared and cannot let go. The final tragic incident is triggered by Curley's wife offering him her hair to touch, and her panicked reaction to his grip on it.

If Lennie existed in real life today, he would be cared for in a sheltered environment where he might learn to manage his strength or where his opportunities to exercise it would be limited. On the face of it, therefore, his strength is his downfall, but the real problem is his lack of control over it a hostile world.

WHAT'S SO GOOD ABOUT THIS ESSAY?

1 Shows firm grasp of question.
2 Good points well argued.
3 Understanding of character.
4 Thorough knowledge of text.
5 Understanding of background and relationships.
6 Perceptive; gives clear answer to question.
7 Awareness of literary devices.
8 Awareness of reader response.
9 Awareness of structure.
10 Apt quotation.

More questions and answers

On pages 74 and 75 you will find two more possible exam questions with Mind Maps and outline answers.

When you have studied them, try writing an outline and a Mind Map for each of the questions below, then compare notes with a friend who has done the same.

1 Examine Steinbeck's treatment of the theme of inequality in *Of Mice and Men*.
2 All humans need friendship and respect. Do you agree?
3 Compare and contrast the opening and closing scenes of *Of Mice and Men*.

QUESTION

How important is Slim in *Of Mice and Men*?

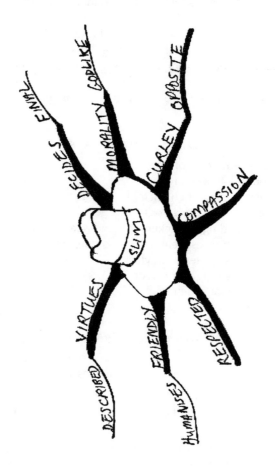

OUTLINE

1 Description of him (full of praise).
2 Humanizes bunkhouse, befriends George and Lennie; gives pup.
3 Respected by all, even Curley (give examples).
4 Final word in everything (Candy's dog, Lennie to die).
5 Sets moral tone (godlike, ageless).
6 Curley represents evil. Slim cannot compete in final event.
7 Compassionate.

QUESTION

John Steinbeck's style in *Of Mice and Men* is more dramatic than descriptive. Do you agree?

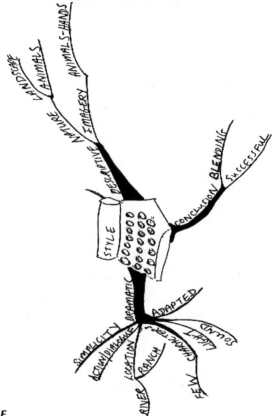

OUTLINE

1 Dramatic style intended – also descriptive.
   - short and simple.
   - crisp dialogue and actions develop story (not thoughts).
   - only two locations (stage directions).
   - few characters, physical descriptions given.
   - frequent mention of lighting (sound effects).
   - later adapted into play.
2 Descriptive writing too.
   - landscape and nature.
   - imagery (animals, hands).
3 Conclusion – successful blending of styles.

GLOSSARY OF LITERARY TERMS

alliteration   repetition of a sound at the beginnings of words; for example, *burn, bubble*.

colloquial   (of language) ordinary, familiar, informal.

context   the social and historical influences on the author; the meaning given to a word or phrase according to its position within other words or phrases.

descriptive   (of style) writing that describes in order to create a mood, but that is not essential to the plot; for example, the beginning of *Of Mice and Men*.

device   the particular way in which a writer achieves an aim without making it obvious; for example, Steinbeck reveals important information through Candy's gossip.

dramatic   (of style) writing in which the story is moved on largely by dialogue.

foreshadowing   an indirect warning of things to come, often through **imagery**; for example, Curley's wife blocking out the light as she enters the bunkhouse.

image   a word picture used to make an idea come alive; for example, a **metaphor**, **simile**, or **personification** (see separate entries).

imagery   the kind of word picture used to make an idea come alive.

irony   the effect achieved when the opposite of what is really meant is said, or when something turns out in the opposite way to what is intended, or to what seems fitting, as if fate were mocking those involved.

metaphor   a description of a thing as if it were something essentially different but also in some way similar; for example, *A silent head and beak lanced down* (the heron's beak is sharp and fast-moving, like a lance).

parody   a comic, exaggerated, or belittling imitation.

personification   a description of something abstract as if it were a person.

realism   a literary style that includes ordinary, everyday details, and in which characters speak and behave as they might do in real life.

setting   the place in which the action occurs, which usually affects the atmosphere; for example, the peaceful spot by the river where *Of Mice and Men* begins and ends.

simile   a comparison of two things that are different in most ways but similar in one important way; for example, *Lennie snorting into the water like a horse.*

slang   nonstandard use of language; for example, *canned* for "sacked."

smallholding   a small piece of land owned and cultivated by laborers to supplement their income.

structure   the organization of the plot.

symbol   an object used by a writer to represent something abstract; for example, the winding Salinas River could be a symbol of life's winding path.

theme   an idea explored by an author, such as friendship.

third person   the kind of narrative in which the author writes as an observer ("He did, she did," and so on)

viewpoint   how the story is told; for example, through action, or in discussion between minor characters.

GLOSSARY OF JARGON

bindle bundle

blackjack card game

blowin' our jack spending our savings

booby-hatch mental hospital

brush-line where small trees and brushes begin

buckin' grain loading grain in sacks

bucks dollars

buggy small horsedrawn carriage

bum steer false information

bums tramps, hoboes

bunkhouse communal shed for sleeping

burlap ticking thick canvas covers on bedding

canned sacked

cat-house brothel

coyote kind of prairie wolf, with a howling cry

crack sex

euchre card game

flapper mouth

flop sex

goo-goos "good government"; people who want to reform things

greybacks lice

hame a piece of wood or metal in a horsecollar

horse-shoe game throwing horseshoes to land around a peg in the ground

hoose-gows   prisons

jail-bait   woman who will get a man into trouble

jerkline   rope connecting the leading horse or mule with the brake, and held by the driver

keg   barrel

kewpie-doll   child's doll with a ponytail

lynched   hanged by a mob before a trial

mules   backless slippers

mutt   mongrel dog

on the county   dependent on social security

pants rabbits   lice

pendula   the plural of pendulum pulp magazine – cheap sensational magazine

punk   unreliable, no-good young person

roaches   cockroaches

roll your hoop   go and play children's games

rummy   card game

San Quentin   top security prison

skinner   driver of teams of horses and mules

slough   throw off

stable buck   man employed to look after horses and mules

Stetson   wide-brimmed cowboy hat

stiffs   tramps, hoboes

swamper   cleaner

thrashin' machine   machine for threshing, cleaning grain

Weed   a town in northern California

wheelers' butt   the backside of the leading horse

whing-ding   an outing; a good time

yella-jackets   wasps, hornets

NDEX